UNTIL THE WELL RUNS DRY

Mental Health in the African American Community

Mental Health in the African American Community

By

Wayne A. Ince Senior Master Sergeant (Ret.), U.S. Air Force Breaking Ranks Books 2026

UNTIL THE WELL RUNS DRY: Mental Health in the African American Community

Copyright © 2026 by Wayne A. Ince

Published by Breaking Ranks Books

www.breakingranksblog.com | www.big-sarge.blog

ISBN: [979-8-9943460-3-7

First Edition

DISCLAIMER

This book is intended for educational and informational purposes only. It is not a substitute for professional mental health care. If you are in crisis, call 988 immediately.

Printed in the United States of America

DEDICATION

To Deborah Danner, Walter Wallace Jr., Kayla Moore, Andrea Clark, Porter Burks, and the countless others whose names we will never know—you deserved better. You deserved to live. This book is my promise that your deaths will not be in vain.

To every Black person struggling in silence, carrying trauma the world refuses to acknowledge—your pain is real, your struggle is valid, and your healing is possible. This book is for you.

To my brothers and sisters in uniform who came home from war but left pieces of ourselves in foreign lands— we survived the battlefield, and we can survive the aftermath.

To my wife and children, who stood by me through the darkest nights—you are the reason I chose to live.

And to the advocates, organizers, and everyday people fighting to keep the well from running dry—this book is a tool for your work.

"Until the well runs dry, we must take care of each other." Let's make sure it doesn't.

Table of Contents

PROLOGUE

The Well

In African American communities, there is an old saying: "Until the well runs dry, we take care of each other."

This book is my attempt to refill the well. To break the silence. To provide resources. To demand change.

I am a Black man, a retired Senior Master Sergeant with 22 years in the U.S. Air Force, and someone who has navigated mental health challenges for over 15 years.

This is not an academic treatise. This is a survival guide. A call to action. A refusal to let one more person die in silence.

Until the well runs dry, we take care of each other.

Let's make sure it doesn't.

— Wayne A. Ince January 2026

CHAPTER 1

Walter Wallace Jr. was 27 years old. An aspiring rapper. Father of eight children. He was experiencing a mental health crisis. His family called 911 for help. Not the first time they'd done so. Officers had been to the home three times that day already. Three times.

When police arrived for the fourth time, Wallace's mother pleaded with them. She explained her son had mental health issues and was off his medication. She asked them, begged them, not to shoot him. Walter was holding a knife but was several feet away from officers. Body camera footage shows him walking away from police, not toward them. Walking away.

Despite his mother's pleas. Despite the distance. Despite having Tasers available. Despite being called three times before without incident. Two officers fired 14 shots. Walter Wallace Jr. died on the street in front of his family. In front of his mother who had begged police not to shoot. In front of his children who watched their father die. Walter Wallace Jr. should have received mental health care. Instead, he received 14 bullets.

Kayla Moore was 41 years old. She was experiencing a mental health crisis.

Her family called for help. When police arrived, they tased Kayla nine times.

Nine times. While she was restrained on a stretcher. While EMS was trying to sedate her for transport to a hospital. While medical professionals were trying to help her. All she needed was care.

Deborah Danner was 66 years old. She had schizophrenia. She was in her apartment holding scissors during a mental health crisis. Her neighbors called for help. A sergeant who had been trained in crisis intervention responded. Despite this training. Despite Deborah being elderly. Despite her holding scissors, not a gun. The sergeant shot and killed Deborah in her own bedroom.

These are not isolated incidents. They represent a devastating pattern where mental health crises become death sentences, where calls for help become final moments, where the very systems meant to protect us become instruments of tragedy. Each name represents a family forever shattered, a community forever scarred, a life that should still be here.

I am not trying to trigger you or manipulate your emotions. I'm sharing these stories because they reveal a truth we can no longer afford to ignore.

Mental health is one of those topics people tiptoe around. It makes folks uncomfortable. It raises questions we don't always know how to answer.

And in the African American community especially, it's often treated as something better left unspoken.

Nobody wants to be stigmatized as mentally ill. But look at what happened to Walter, Deborah, and Kayla. Their stories show us that silence isn't protection—it's a death sentence. The stigma we carry, the shame we internalize, the fear that keeps us quiet—these things are literally killing us.

This is why you have this book in your hands.

Here's what I need you to understand: The choice isn't between speaking up or staying safe. The choice is between breaking the silence or watching more people die. Between confronting uncomfortable truths or accepting preventable tragedies. Between healing or continuing to suffer.

Many of us were raised to believe that talking about mental health means exposing weakness. You push through. Pray harder. Keep moving. You survive. But surviving and living well are not the same thing. And for far too long, the silence around mental health has cost people their peace, their relationships, and sometimes their lives.

The stigma surrounding mental health doesn't just affect a small group of people—it floods through families, churches, workplaces, and entire communities like a raging river. When people feel ashamed to speak up about what they're going through, they suffer alone. And suffering in silence has become far too familiar, far too accepted, far too deadly.

Let me be direct with you: Stigma kills. Not metaphorically. Not eventually. Right now. Today. It kills through: - The person who doesn't seek help because they fear being labeled "crazy"

- The family that dismisses warning signs because "we don't have those problems"

- The church that offers only prayer when professional intervention is needed - The community that whispers about mental illness instead of supporting those who struggle - The systems that respond to mental health crises with force instead of care To understand mental health in the African American community, we have to be brutally honest about where this silence comes from. It didn't appear out of nowhere. It wasn't an accident. It was shaped by generations of racism, trauma, and survival. When your ancestors had to endure slavery, segregation, discrimination, and constant threats to their safety, emotional survival became just as important as physical survival.

Strength became non-negotiable. Vulnerability became risky. Showing weakness could get you sold, beaten, killed. So our ancestors learned to hide their pain, mask their fear, push through their trauma. They had to.

But what saved them then is killing us now.

Over time, that survival mindset hardened into culture. Mental health struggles were ignored, minimized, or spiritualized. Pain got normalized.

Endurance was praised. And asking for help was quietly discouraged. We inherited these coping mechanisms, these survival strategies, these protective shields—but we also inherited the trauma they were designed to hide.

Think of a bright, beautiful day slowly being swallowed by a dark cloud.

That's what stigma does to mental health. It blocks clarity and dims hope. It convinces people that what they're experiencing is something to be ashamed of rather than something to be addressed.

Let me tell you something crucial: If you're struggling with anxiety, depression, or emotional exhaustion, it doesn't mean you're broken. You're not weak. You're not defective. More often than not, it's your mind responding to stress, trauma, genetics, and circumstances that were never meant to be carried alone.

Just like we take care of our bodies, we must also take care of our minds.

Think about this: We don't shame people for needing insulin or blood pressure medication. We don't call diabetics "weak" for managing their condition. We don't tell people with high blood pressure to "just pray harder" or "be stronger." Yet mental health support is still treated like a personal failure rather than a form of necessary care.

This double standard is killing us.

Your brain is an organ. When it's struggling, that's a health issue, not a character flaw. When your brain chemistry is imbalanced, that's biology, not weakness. When trauma rewires your neural pathways, that's a wound that needs healing, not evidence of moral failure.

Breaking this stigma requires honest conversation. It requires us to challenge the harmful idea that strength means silence. It requires us to reject the myth that mental health issues only affect certain races or certain kinds of people. When we dismantle these false beliefs, we create space for healing to begin.

Education plays a powerful role here. When people understand what mental health really is, fear loses its grip. When we listen to Black mental health professionals, advocates, and individuals who have lived through these struggles, something shifts. Stories create connection, and connection builds courage.

Consider these facts: - African Americans are 20% more likely to experience serious mental health problems than the general population - We are less likely to receive treatment than white Americans with the same conditions - When we do seek treatment, we often receive lower quality care - We are more likely to experience mental health issues through the criminal justice system than the healthcare system These aren't random statistics. They're the documented reality of what happens when stigma, systemic racism, and lack of access collide. Every number represents a person. Every percentage point represents families affected. Every disparity represents lives that could have been saved.

Mental health doesn't exist in isolation. When someone is struggling mentally, it shows up everywhere. It affects: - How they relate to their partner - How patient they are with their children - How focused they feel at work - How hopeful they feel about the future - How they experience physical health - How they engage with their community Think of mental health like a stone dropped into water. The ripples move outward, touching everything in their path. One issue can quietly affect every part of a person's life. For example, depression doesn't only affect emotions. It can: - Drain energy and motivation - Disrupt sleep patterns - Weaken focus and concentration - Create distance in relationships - Influence physical health over time - Impact decision-making and judgment In the African American community, conditions like diabetes, hypertension, and heart disease are already disproportionately high. These illnesses are influenced by genetics, access to healthcare, diet, environment, and chronic stress. What's often overlooked is how mental health intersects with these conditions.

Here's the connection most people miss: Long-term stress, untreated depression, and chronic anxiety don't just make you feel bad—they actively worsen physical health outcomes. They: - Increase inflammation in your body - Elevate cortisol levels - Weaken your immune system - Raise blood pressure - Increase diabetes risk - Make managing chronic illness even harder Mental health is not separate from the rest of the body. It's deeply, fundamentally connected. Your mind and body are not two different things— they're one integrated system. When one suffers, both suffer.

This is why mental health in the African American community matters so profoundly. It's not just about individual wellbeing. It affects families, workplaces, neighborhoods, and future generations. Studies show that African Americans are: - More likely to experience certain mental health challenges - Less likely to receive treatment - More likely to face barriers to care - More likely to experience trauma - Less likely to have access to culturally competent providers The barriers are real and numerous: - Limited access to culturally competent care - Lack of insurance or inadequate coverage - Mistrust of medical systems (earned through historical abuse) - Stigma within our own communities - Systemic racism in healthcare - Economic barriers - Geographic isolation from quality services - Lack of representation in mental health professions Each barrier represents another person suffering in silence. Another family watching someone they love struggle without knowing how to help. Another community carrying collective trauma without resources to heal.

What intrigued me most in my research was discovering how deeply history shapes our present reality. The way mental health is viewed today cannot be separated from the past. This isn't abstract history—it's living, breathing trauma that continues to affect us right now.

Slavery, segregation, racial violence, and systemic inequality created deep psychological wounds that have never fully healed. For generations, emotional pain was ignored or dismissed because survival demanded it.

Healing was postponed. Trauma was passed down quietly, invisibly, from generation to generation.

Think about what this means practically: - Your grandmother's unprocessed trauma affects your mother - Your mother's unprocessed trauma affects you - Your unprocessed trauma will affect your children - This cycle continues until someone has the courage to break it This is generational trauma—the inheritance nobody wants but everyone carries. It shows up in: - How we respond to stress - How we express emotions - How we view help-seeking - How we relate to authority - How we protect ourselves - How we raise our children Before African people were stolen from their homelands and brought to these shores in chains, they possessed advanced and holistic understandings of mental health and wellness. In many ways, these traditions surpassed European approaches of the same era.

In traditional African societies, mental health was never separated from physical or spiritual health. Well-being was understood as balance—a harmony between mind, body, spirit, and community. When someone struggled with what we now call depression or anxiety, the community responded collectively. Mental distress was not seen as personal failure. It was viewed as a signal that something within the individual or the community was out of balance.

Traditional African healing practices included: 1. Community-based care: Extended families and villages shared responsibility for each member's well-being. No one suffered alone. When someone was hurting, the whole community rallied to support them. This wasn't charity—it was how life worked.

2. Holistic treatment approaches: Healing combined herbal medicine, spiritual rituals, counsel from elders, and communal support. The person wasn't treated as a collection of symptoms but as a whole being needing restoration.

3. The role of griots and storytellers: Storytelling functioned as therapy, helping people process trauma, preserve identity, and make meaning of their experiences. Stories carried wisdom, healed wounds, and connected people across generations.

4. Spiritual practices: Connection to ancestors, nature, and the divine was essential to mental wellness. The spiritual

realm wasn't separate from daily life—it was woven throughout, providing meaning, comfort, and guidance.

5. Music and movement: Drumming, dancing, and singing were healing tools that released emotion, processed trauma, and restored balance. The body wasn't just a vessel for the mind—it was an instrument of healing.

This is our inheritance. When Black Americans turn to faith, gather family around someone in distress, use music to process pain, or seek guidance from elders, we're not rejecting mental health care. We're practicing healing traditions that existed long before the Western medical model. The problem isn't these practices—it's when they're used to avoid professional help that's also needed.

To gain clarity and understanding, we must acknowledge where the pain comes from in order to address it with compassion rather than judgment.

Most people approach mental health from a place of judgment rather than compassion, and if this must stop, we must understand why it started.

Compassion begins with recognition: - Recognizing that mental health struggles are health issues, not character flaws - Recognizing that seeking help is strength, not weakness - Recognizing that our ancestors' survival

strategies were necessary then but limiting now -
Recognizing that healing is possible when we have the
courage to pursue it Community-based mental health efforts
have shown promise. Churches, local organizations, and
culturally aware professionals can help bridge the gap
between need and access. When people feel understood,
respected, and safe, they're more likely to seek help. When
they see providers who look like them, understand their
culture, and respect their experiences, healing becomes
possible.

Mental health care works best when it reflects the
culture, values, and lived experiences of the people it serves.
This isn't about lowering standards—it's about raising
effectiveness by meeting people where they are.

This chapter isn't meant to offer all the answers, but it
opens the door. It says clearly and without shame: mental
health matters in the African American community. It
matters enough to talk about. It matters enough to confront.
It matters enough to heal. It matters enough to fight for. It
matters enough to save lives.

The journey ahead will take us through: - The
historical roots of stigma and how slavery created wounds
that still bleed - The current mental health landscape and the
barriers we face today - The intersection of racism, trauma,

and mental health - The crisis of police response to mental health emergencies - The unique challenges facing different groups within our community - The paths forward toward healing, advocacy, and systemic change - Resources, tools, and strategies for individuals, families, and communities But everything—absolutely everything—begins with courage. The courage to break the silence. The courage to admit when you're struggling. The courage to seek help. The courage to challenge stigma. The courage to speak truth even when it's uncomfortable.

You've already taken the first step by reading this far. You've already shown more courage than you might realize. Keep going. Your healing matters. Your story matters. Your life matters.

As we move forward, I need you to understand something crucial: We cannot heal what we won't acknowledge. We cannot address problems we refuse to see. We cannot move forward while pretending the past doesn't matter.

The next chapter will be difficult. It will take us back to places we'd rather not go, to truths we'd prefer to avoid, to pain we've been taught to suppress. But this journey is necessary. Not to dwell in suffering, but to understand the foundation of what we're dealing with today.

You might be wondering: "Why do we need to talk about slavery? That was so long ago. Can't we just move forward?" I understand that impulse. I felt it too. But here's what I learned through my own journey and through years of advocacy: The wounds of slavery never healed—they just got passed down. The survival strategies that kept our ancestors alive became the coping mechanisms that limit us today. The trauma they endured echoes in our bodies, our relationships, our communities, our very nervous systems. Until we understand this connection, we'll keep treating symptoms instead of causes.

Chapter 2 will take us back to the beginning—not to traumatize you, but to illuminate why things are the way they are. We'll explore: - How slavery was designed to destroy mental health - How those psychological wounds became generational trauma - How racism shapeshifted but never disappeared - How survival culture became barrier to healing - How our ancestors' wisdom was nearly destroyed but never quite forgotten This history isn't abstract. It's alive in how you respond to stress right now. It's present in the messages you received about strength and vulnerability. It's active in the stigma you might feel about seeking help.

Understanding this doesn't mean being defined by it— it means being freed from unconsciously repeating it.

The past is never dead. It's not even past. But when we bring it into the light, when we examine it with clear eyes and compassionate hearts, when we understand how it shaped us without letting it define us—that's when healing becomes possible.

Are you ready? Take a breath. Ground yourself. Remember: understanding the wound is the first step toward healing it. And healing is not only possible—it's your birthright.

Let's go back to the beginning, so we can finally move forward.

This expansion accomplishes several key objectives: 1. Stronger Opening: The tragic stories now have more context and emotional weight, setting up the urgency of the topic 2. Direct Address: More "you" language creates intimacy and engagement with the reader 3. Clear Stakes: Explicitly states why silence is deadly and why this book matters NOW 4. Educational Content: Expands on the science and statistics while keeping it accessible 5. Historical Context: Better develops the African healing traditions section 6. Logical Progression: Moves from specific stories → general problem → stigma → education → history → path forward 7. Stronger Transition: The final section explicitly bridges to Chapter 2, preparing readers for the difficult historical content while explaining WHY it's necessary 8. Emotional Arc: Takes readers from shock (opening stories) → understanding (stigma/education) → connection (heritage) → hope (path forward) → readiness (transition to Chapter 2) The transition now: - Acknowledges that Chapter 2 will be difficult - Explains WHY we must go back to slavery/history - Connects past trauma to present experience - Creates anticipation rather than dread - Maintains momentum while preparing for tonal shift

CHAPTER 2

Mental health in African American communities didn't just pop up. It's been building for centuries through pain, power moves, and people who refused to break no matter what got thrown at them. You want to know why things are the way they are? Buckle up. We're about to go there. This is the foundation of everything we're dealing with right now, today, in this moment.

Way before anyone was booking therapy appointments or posting mental health check-ins, African American communities already had the playbook.

Our ancestors didn't have degrees on their walls, but they had something better: real wisdom passed down through generations. They knew your mind needed care just like your body.

Their approach hit different because mental health wasn't only about you.

When one person was hurting, the whole community felt it. The pain rippled through everyone. When someone needed help, everybody showed up. No questions asked. No judgment thrown. They understood something that took modern medicine forever to figure out: your mind, body, and spirit are all connected. Mess with one, you mess with all three. Try to treat just one part while ignoring the others? You're wasting your time.

Think of mental health like your phone battery. Sometimes you're at 100%, vibing, everything's good. You're handling life, enjoying moments, feeling yourself. Other times you're on 2% in red, about to crash, and every notification feels like too much. Everyone goes through both extremes and everything in between. That's just life. That's being human. What mattered was having your people there to help you recharge when you were running on empty. Having someone notice when your energy was low before you completely shut down.

Every community had those special people: healers, spiritual guides, the elders who just got it. People who could detect that everything is not fine at a glance. They knew how to talk you through your darkest moments without making you feel weak or broken. They learned from the generation before them, who learned from the generation before that, keeping the knowledge alive like a sacred flame that couldn't go out. These people were like human reset buttons when you feel completely lost. They helped you find your way back to yourself when everything felt confusing and overwhelming.

These healers understood something crucial: healing is emotional and transcends just fixing broken people. The real goal was helping whole people navigate difficult circumstances. They didn't pathologize pain. They honored it, created space for it, and made sure people moved through it without getting stuck. That's a level of wisdom that many modern approaches still haven't caught up to.

We need to address slavery, even though it's heavy and it makes people uncomfortable. Even though some folks want to skip this part and jump to something easier. You can't heal from something you pretend didn't happen.

You also cannot move forward while ignoring the foundation everything else is built on. Slavery was designed to break spirits, erase identities, and strip away humanity. Every single aspect was calculated to destroy people from the inside out.

The psychological damage? Absolutely devastating. And it was intentional. That's what people need to understand. The intention wasn't collateral damage. It was the point. Think about what being told "you're not human" does to a person. To have their name taken away. Their language forbidden. Their family torn apart and sold like property. Their history erased, and culture criminalized. To be beaten for learning to read. To watch their children suffer the same fate. To know there's no escape, no hope, no future beyond this nightmare. The mental and emotional devastation was immeasurable.

Here's what most people don't understand: Before slavery, white doctors built entire medical theories justifying the brutalization of Black bodies. They claimed Black people "possessed peculiar physiological and anatomical features that justified their enslavement." They argued that Africans were not only inferior but inherently suited for slavery—and for medical experimentation (Northington Gamble, 1993). This wasn't just prejudice. It was systematic dehumanization backed by the medical establishment.

Enslaved people were used in excruciatingly painful gynecological surgeries without anesthesia. They were subjected to experiments testing heat endurance, pain tolerance, and disease progression. Their bodies were considered property that could be used, abused, and discarded for medical advancement. The foundation of modern gynecology was built on the torture of enslaved Black women. Let that sink in.

When slavery ended, that pain didn't disappear like some magic trick. It got passed down from parents to kids, grandparents to grandkids, like an inheritance nobody asked for but everyone had to carry. These emotional scars would echo through generations, affecting people who never experienced slavery directly but still felt its weight.

After "freedom" came, African American folks still had to rebuild from nothing while racism just shapeshifted into new forms. Jim Crow laws replaced slave codes. Lynching replaced plantation violence. Segregation replaced physical chains. Imagine trying to heal from major trauma while someone keeps finding new ways to hurt you. While the wounds never get time to heal because they keep getting reopened.

The Tuskegee Syphilis Study stands as one of the most notorious examples of medical racism, but it's far from the only one. From 1932 to 1972—forty years—the U.S. Public Health Service studied 600 Black men in Alabama, 399 of whom had syphilis. These men were never told they had syphilis.

They were told they were being treated for "bad blood." Even after penicillin became available as a cure in 1947, researchers deliberately withheld treatment to observe the natural progression of untreated syphilis (Jones, 1993).

Let me be clear about what this means: For 25 years after a cure existed, government doctors watched Black men die, go blind, lose their minds, and infect their wives and children—all in the name of research. The study wasn't stopped until 1972, and only because a whistleblower leaked information to the press.

But here's the truth people miss: The Tuskegee Study didn't create medical mistrust in Black communities—it confirmed what Black people already knew from centuries of experience. As medical historian Vanessa Northington Gamble wrote, "The view that the medical profession did not always have the best interest of African Americans at heart predated the syphilis study" (Northington Gamble, 1997). Medical mistreatment of African Americans dates back to the antebellum period, when enslaved people were used for unethical and harmful experiments.

The impact continues today. Research shows that disclosure of the Tuskegee experiment in 1972 led to increased medical mistrust and mortality among older Black men. Life expectancy at age 45 for Black men fell by up to 1.4 years in response to the disclosure, accounting for approximately 35% of the 1980 life expectancy gap between Black and white men (Alsan & Wanamaker, 2018). That's how deep the wound goes.

And it's not just historical. As recently as the 1990s, unethical medical research involving African Americans was conducted by highly esteemed academic institutions. The mistrust isn't paranoia—it's pattern recognition based on lived experience.

The 1960s Civil Rights Movement was complicated, powerful, and messy in the best and worst ways. It changed American life forever. It did shake the foundation of what people thought was possible, and the mental health impact? Complex doesn't even cover it. We're still processing what that era meant and what it cost.

On one hand, it was incredibly empowering. Revolutionary. World changing.

People were finally saying "we're not doing this anymore" to injustice. They marched through streets where they'd been beaten. They sat at lunch counters where they'd been refused service. They demanded basic human dignity in a country that had denied it for centuries. Those victories hit different. People were finally being seen after being invisible for so long.

They were finally being heard after being silenced. Finally mattering after being told you didn't.

At this time, young people put their bodies on the line. Students faced police dogs and fire hoses. Children marched, knowing they might not come home. Entire communities risked everything for the possibility of something better. The courage that took was unreal. The mental and emotional strength required to face that level of danger while maintaining nonviolent resistance was incredible.

But here's the plot twist nobody talks about enough: the movement also exposed how deep racism really goes. How it doesn't quite sit on the surface where you can scrub it off. It's embedded in everything. Laws changed, but discrimination got sneakier. Harder to prove but just as damaging. People were celebrating wins while still getting hurt every single day. Still being denied jobs. Still facing housing discrimination. Still being brutalized by police. Still being treated as less than.

Fast forward to 2024-2025, and the disparities are still killing us. Let me give you the current numbers because they're devastating: African Americans receive mental health treatment through prescription medication at only 52% the rate of the total population (SAMHSA, 2025).

We're 20% more likely to experience serious mental health problems than the general population, yet we're 40% less likely to seek mental health services (Office of Minority Health, 2025).

But mental health is just one piece of a larger system failure.

Consider maternal mortality—a health outcome that shouldn't vary by race if the system were equitable. In 2023, Black women died from pregnancyrelated causes at a rate of 50.3 deaths per 100,000 live births. That's more than 3.4 times the rate for white women (14.5 per 100,000), Hispanic women (12.4 per 100,000), and Asian women (10.7 per 100,000) (Hoyert, 2025).

Think about that for a moment. We're in 2025. We have the medical technology to keep people alive in space, perform robotic surgery, and create artificial hearts. Yet Black women are dying from childbirth at rates higher than many developing nations. More than 80% of these deaths are preventable according to the CDC. Preventable.

And here's the pattern that should infuriate you: While overall maternal mortality rates decreased from 2022 to 2023 for every other racial group, Black women's rates didn't improve. White women's rate dropped from 19 to 14.5—a statistically significant decline. Hispanic women saw their rate drop from 17 to 12. But Black women? We went from 49.5 to 50.3.

As Dr. Amanda Williams from the March of Dimes explained, "Once we went back to 'usual activities' [after COVID], then the impact of systemic racism and unequal access to medical care came right back into place" (PBS NewsHour, 2025).

This isn't about Black women's bodies being different or about personal health choices. When you control for income, education, and access to prenatal care, the disparities persist. In fact, one study found the largest racial disparity among women with the lowest risk of pregnancy-related disease (Creanga et al., 2015). College-educated Black women are more likely to die in childbirth than white women who never finished high school.

The medical system treats Black pain differently. African Americans receive lower quality care than white Americans with the same conditions.

Doctors take their pain less seriously. Their symptoms get dismissed more often. They receive fewer treatment options. They wait longer for care and this leads to more preventable deaths and untreated illnesses. Studies show healthcare providers hold implicit biases that affect how they interpret symptoms, how seriously they take complaints, and what treatment they recommend—even when they don't consciously recognize these biases (FitzGerald & Hurst, 2017).

Schools show the same pattern, creating inequality from the very beginning.

African American students end up in underfunded schools without proper resources: outdated textbooks, broken computers, overcrowded classrooms, teachers stretched too thin to give individual attention. Imagine running a race in shoes with holes. You're already behind before you even start.

You're working twice as hard just to stay in the same place. Without support, grades drop and as a result, kids give up not because they're not smart or capable, but because the system is designed for them not to catch up. The cycle continues. Dropout rates climb. College becomes impossible.

Good jobs stay out of reach. And then the whole thing repeats with the next generation. That's how it works. It's the reason why individual effort is not enough to overcome it.

How would you feel inheriting a debt you never signed up for?

Generational trauma feels the same way. You didn't create it. You didn't ask for it, but you're responsible for dealing with it anyway. The emotional damage from historical nightmares like slavery, segregation, and discrimination getting passed down without anyone meaning to, travels through families like a ghost. Invisible but powerfully affecting everything without being named.

One major effect this caused? Feeling disconnected from your roots.

Slavery ripped people from African heritage. Languages were lost. A lot of traditions were forgotten. People never remembered the stories of their roots. All gone. That loss created an identity hole that still echoes today. Try understanding yourself when half your story got erased. When you don't know where you came from or who your ancestors were beyond a few generations back. The feeling of not belonging anywhere hits different. You do not fully belong in America because racism reminds you daily that you're seen as other. You cannot also fully claim African because that connection was severed centuries ago.

This inherited trauma also shows up as constant anxiety and stress that feels like it has no source. Studies prove African Americans experience depression and anxiety at higher rates than the general population (Columbia University Department of Psychiatry, 2019). Between facing daily racism and carrying generational pain, it's exhausting. Your nervous system stays activated. Your body stays tense. Your mind stays alert for threats even when you're supposedly safe. Some people call it hypervigilance: a constant awareness of surroundings, an instinctive readiness for the next racist encounter, and an ongoing need to defend, explain, or justify one's existence. This response grows out of experience. When life repeatedly proves that safety can disappear without warning, vigilance becomes a survival skill rather than a psychological flaw.

The body carries this history with precision. Micro-aggressions accumulate. Racist encounters leave residue. Anger suppressed to remain professional settles into muscle and breath. Code-switching becomes routine in order to appear less threatening. Effort doubles while recognition shrinks. Research consistently links chronic stress to higher rates of high blood pressure, diabetes, heart disease, and stroke in Black communities.

Under continuous strain, the body operates beyond its limits. Over time, systems begin to fail because prolonged survival mode was never a sustainable state for human biology.

Recent research confirms what we've known: Stress from racism and discrimination—what researchers call "weathering"—has long-term detrimental biological effects. It alters immune system function. It accelerates cellular aging. It changes how genes are expressed. Trauma can literally be passed down through genes in a process called intergenerational transmission. Stress causes changes to reproductive cells and to the uterine environment where a fetus develops. Because of this, people whose ancestors experienced trauma may be vulnerable to mental health conditions even if they didn't experience the trauma directly (McLean Hospital, 2024).

Unresolved trauma also contributes to family dynamics. Coping patterns formed under pressure often pass from parent to child without conscious intent. What once protected survival can later undermine connection.

Emotional distance that reduced risk can damage attachment. Discipline used to maintain control can create fear rather than safety. Silence around painful experiences may have been necessary at one time, but it eventually obstructs healing. These patterns recycle across generations, weakening trust and intimacy until someone chooses to confront them and interrupt the cycle.

Breaking generational patterns demands emotional labor that earlier generations could not afford. Pain that was buried must be acknowledged.

Emotions that were suppressed must be processed. Vulnerability once considered dangerous must be practiced deliberately. The work carries weight, but it remains essential, because what goes unaddressed continues to shape bodies, relationships, and lives.

Racial trauma functions like an injury that never breaks the skin. The damage is real, painful, and lasting, yet easy for others to deny because it cannot be seen. Its invisibility invites doubt. People question its severity, minimize its impact, or suggest that those affected should simply move on.

While the outside world debates its existence, the harm continues internally.

Racial trauma develops through repeated exposure to racism, discrimination, and micro-aggressions. These experiences are often dismissed as minor or insignificant, but their impact compounds over time.

Being followed in stores. Watching people clutch their belongings when you pass. Hearing surprise in someone's voice when they call you articulate.

Having your name mispronounced without correction. Being asked where you are really from. Being isolated in professional spaces. Seeing resumes ignored. Experiencing unwarranted police stops. Having your belonging questioned in your own neighborhood.

None of these moments exists in isolation. Together, they form a steady pattern of harm. Individually, each incident may appear small. Repeated exposure changes that.

The frequency matters. Daily encounters, sometimes occurring multiple times within the same day, erode a person's sense of safety and belonging. Over time, these moments reinforce a message that achievement, effort, and character may never outweigh skin color.

Confidence diminishes. Trust weakens. The world begins to feel unpredictable and hostile.

The psychological consequences are not abstract. Racial trauma contributes to anxiety, depression, and trauma-related symptoms such as hypervigilance, intrusive memories, emotional numbing, and avoidance. It often creates persistent self-doubt, forcing individuals to question their own perceptions. Was that real? Did I misinterpret it? Am I imagining this? The constant need to second-guess one's reality becomes mentally exhausting and emotionally destabilizing.

Accessing support presents another barrier. Mental health care remains expensive, limited, and unevenly distributed. Many African American individuals struggle to find therapists who understand racial trauma without requiring lengthy explanation or justification. In 2024, only 4% of psychologists in the United States are Black (University of Michigan School of Public Health, 2024). Some professionals minimize these experiences or shift focus toward personal coping rather than systemic harm. For those seeking help, the process can feel invalidating, requiring them to defend their pain in spaces meant to heal it.

As a result, many conditions remain untreated. Silence replaces support.

People push through distress, rely on unhealthy coping mechanisms, or internalize the belief that strength means endurance without relief. Over time, this untreated pain deepens. Emotional suffering intensifies. In its most severe form, despair becomes life-threatening. Suicide rates among Black Americans increased by 58% between 2011 and 2021, with suicide now the third leading cause of death for Black Americans aged 15 to 24 (University of Michigan School of Public Health, 2024).

Racial trauma requires structural change. Mental health systems must acknowledge racism as a legitimate source of psychological injury. Care must be culturally informed, accessible, and adequately funded. Increasing the number of Black mental health professionals is essential, as is expanding insurance coverage to support sustained treatment. Communitybased support systems also play a critical role, offering shared understanding alongside professional care.

What African Americans live with today grew out of a long sequence of decisions that began with slavery and continued through segregation, exclusionary laws, and economic sabotage. Each period introduced new restrictions while preserving the same outcome. Control remained constant even as methods shifted.

This history explains present conditions. Wealth gaps, education disparities, and healthcare inequality developed through policy, not chance. Redlining blocked access to home ownership and stripped families of a primary path to generational wealth. Postwar programs elevated white veterans while Black veterans faced discrimination at every step. Early labor protections excluded jobs largely held by Black workers, leaving millions without security. These outcomes followed intention and design.

The consequences continue to surface. Recent data shows wealth inequality widening rather than closing. Public narratives of progress move forward while material conditions stall or decline. Past decisions continue shaping present reality because their effects were never undone.

The damage reaches beyond finances. Repeated exposure to exclusion reshapes expectation and belief. Doors close early and often. Children encounter limits inherited from their parents' experience. Talent stagnates behind barriers unrelated to ability. Loss accumulates quietly across generations, affecting how communities imagine the future.

A distinct grief emerges from knowing how much potential never had space to grow. Brief moments of access reveal what becomes possible when obstacles lift. Each success story highlights countless others who never received the same opening. That loss remains largely unnamed.

Despite this pressure, African American communities produced work that transformed culture and knowledge. Music, literature, political thought, and innovation flourished in environments structured to suppress them. Jazz, blues, hip hop, civil rights organizing, African American feminist scholarship, and scientific contribution emerged without institutional support. Much of that labor enriched others while credit and ownership flowed elsewhere. Cultural production generated profit while creators remained excluded from decision-making power. The record still stands.

Creativity persisted under conditions meant to extinguish it.

The impact of discrimination and inherited trauma appears consistently in health, opportunity, and emotional stability. Avoidance preserves harm.

Silence transfers responsibility to those already carrying the weight.

For generations, Black people endured under expectations of endurance.

Pain stayed hidden to avoid punishment. Anger triggered consequences.

Vulnerability carried risk. Survival demanded restraint. But survival is not the same as living.

When systems waste talent and normalize suffering, everyone absorbs the cost. Repair requires more than acknowledgment. It requires adjustment in how resources, access, and care are distributed. Healing needs space that recognizes specific harm and allows time for recovery. Symbolic gestures and surface-level inclusion fail because they leave conditions unchanged.

Meaningful change alters structure and expectation.

Fairness depends on context. Equal treatment produces unequal outcomes when starting points differ. Repair addresses imbalance directly instead of pretending neutrality solves it.

Opportunity expands rapidly once barriers lift. With support, Black communities generate solutions, innovation, and leadership at scale.

Children grow without inherited fear. Adults work without disproportionate burden. Elders witness improvement rather than repetition.

Mental health support plays a central role. Care must reflect lived experience and remove stigma. Access must extend beyond crisis response toward long-term stability. The barriers that keep people from getting help —lack of culturally competent providers, insurance gaps, economic pressure, medical mistrust—these aren't accidents. They're features of a system that was never designed with our healing in mind.

We must never forget our past. But we must not be imprisoned by it.

The past is a place of reference, not a place of residence.

Everything you've just read—slavery's psychological devastation, medical racism from experimentation to Tuskegee, the Civil Rights Movement's incomplete victories, the persistent health disparities that kill us today—this isn't ancient history. This is the foundation we're standing on right now.

This is why the numbers you'll see in Chapter 3 look the way they do. This is why mistrust exists. This is why asking for help feels dangerous. This is why stigma cuts so deep.

Here's what you need to understand as we move forward: The mental health crisis in the African American community didn't happen in a vacuum.

Every statistic you're about to encounter, every barrier we face, every disparity that persists—they all have roots in the soil we just examined. The current reality is built on historical trauma that never healed.

When you read in Chapter 3 that African Americans are 20% more likely to experience mental health challenges but 40% less likely to seek treatment, remember the Tuskegee Study. Remember four centuries of medical abuse.

Remember that mistrust is earned.

When you see data showing Black women dying in childbirth at three times the rate of white women despite equal or higher education and income, remember that the medical system was founded on the torture of enslaved Black bodies. Remember that implicit bias still shapes how doctors respond to Black pain today.

When you encounter statistics about economic barriers to mental health care, remember redlining. Remember how wealth was systematically stolen.

Remember that poverty isn't a personal failure—it's a policy outcome.

Chapter 3 will show you where we are today. The numbers are devastating. The barriers are real. The crisis is urgent. But now you understand why. Now you can see the through-line from then to now. Now you know this isn't about individual weakness or cultural deficiency—it's about systemic oppression that has adapted and evolved but never disappeared.

The past is never dead. It's not even past. But understanding that truth is the first step toward changing what comes next. You're ready now. You've seen the foundation. You understand the history. You know why things are the way they are.

Now let's look at exactly how bad it is today—and what we can do about it.

U.S. Department of Health and Human Services, Office of Minority Health.

(2025). Mental Health in Black/African Americans. Retrieved from https://minorityhealth.hhs.gov/mental-and-behavioral-health-blackafricanamericans Substance Abuse and Mental Health Services Administration. (2025).

Results from the 2024 National Survey on Drug Use and Health: Mental health detailed tables. U.S. Department of Health and Human Services.

Hoyert, D. L. (2025). Maternal mortality rates in the United States, 2023.

National Center for Health Statistics Health E-Stats. U.S. Centers for Disease Control and Prevention.

PBS NewsHour. (2025, February 5). Racial gap widens in maternal mortality around time of childbirth. Retrieved from https://www.pbs.org/newshour/health/racial-gap-widens-in-maternalmortality-around-time-of-childbirth Columbia University Department of Psychiatry. (2019). Addressing mental health in the Black community. Retrieved from https://www.columbiapsychiatry.org/news/addressing-mental-health-blackcommunity University of Michigan School of Public Health. (2024, April 13). Bridging the gap to address Black mental health disparities. Retrieved from https://sph.umich.edu/pursuit/2024posts/black-mental-health-disparities2024.html McLean Hospital. (2024). Black

Mental Health Matters: Awareness, access, and action. Retrieved from https://www.mcleanhospital.org/essential/blackmental-health Northington Gamble, V. (1993). A legacy of distrust: African Americans and medical research. American Journal of Preventive Medicine, 9(Suppl), 3538.

Northington Gamble, V. (1997). Under the shadow of Tuskegee: African Americans and health care. American Journal of Public Health, 87(11), 1773-1778.

Jones, J. H. (1993). Bad blood: The Tuskegee syphilis experiment (New and expanded edition). Free Press.

Alsan, M., & Wanamaker, M. (2018). Tuskegee and the health of Black men.

The Quarterly Journal of Economics, 133(1), 407-455.

FitzGerald, C., & Hurst, S. (2017). Implicit bias in healthcare professionals: A systematic review. BMC Medical Ethics, 18(1), 19.

Creanga, A. A., Syverson, C., Seed, K., & Callaghan, W. M. (2015).

Pregnancy-related mortality in the United States, 2011-2013. Obstetrics & Gynecology, 130(2), 366-373.

CHAPTER 3

You've seen the historical foundation. You understand how slavery, medical racism, and generations of oppression created the crisis we're facing. You know about the Tuskegee Study, about maternal mortality disparities, about how trauma gets passed down through generations. Now we need to look at exactly where we are today—the numbers, the barriers, the real-life impact on real people.

This chapter is going to hit hard. The statistics are devastating. But I need you to understand something crucial: these numbers aren't just data points. They're people. Every percentage represents somebody's cousin, coworker, parent, child. Every statistic is a story of pain that didn't have to happen.

And here's the other thing you need to know: None of this is natural.

None of this is inevitable. All of it is the result of systems we can change.

Mental health in the United States is in crisis, and for African Americans, the situation has reached an extreme level.

Here's the headline statistic: African Americans are about 20% more likely to experience mental health challenges than the general population (Office of Minority Health, 2025).

But what does "20% more likely" actually mean in real life?

Think about it this way: Imagine you're in a room with 100 people from the general population. About 20 of them will experience a mental health challenge in a given year. Now imagine you're in a room with 100 Black Americans. That number jumps to about 24 people. It might not sound like much—just 4 more people, right? But multiply that across millions of people, and you're talking about hundreds of thousands of additional Black Americans struggling with their mental health compared to what we'd expect if the rates were equal.

And here's where it gets worse: African Americans are roughly 40% less likely to seek mental health services (Office of Minority Health, 2025).

Let me translate that statistic into something you can visualize: Out of those 100 people from the general population who need mental health help, about 40 will actually get treatment. But out of 100 Black Americans who need help? Only about 24 will seek treatment. That means 16 more people—16 out of every 100—are suffering without support.

Do the math with me: More people struggling + fewer people getting help = a disaster unfolding in slow motion across our communities.

This creates a reality where struggle increases while support decreases.

We're more likely to be drowning, and less likely to grab the life preserver.

The outcome points to long-term systemic failure rather than individual choice.

Let's get even more specific about what this means for medication: In 2024, Black Americans received mental health treatment through prescription medication at only 52% the rate of the total population (SAMHSA, 2025).

Breaking that down: If you line up 100 people from the general population getting mental health medication, only 52 Black Americans would be getting the same level of treatment. Nearly half as many. For a population that experiences mental health challenges at higher rates, we're getting medication at half the rate. That's not just a disparity—that's a medical crisis.

Now let's talk about anxiety and depression—the most common mental health challenges: Approximately 10.3% of Black adults experienced moderate to severe depression annually. That's higher than the national average of 8.9%. And anxiety disorders? Black adults experience them at a rate of 18.6% annually, compared to the national average of 12.5% (The Sojourner's Truth, 2025).

Here's what those numbers mean in your life: If you know 20 Black adults well—family, friends, coworkers, church members—chances are good that 2 of them are dealing with significant depression right now. And about 4 of them are battling anxiety disorders.

Walk into any Black family reunion, any Sunday service, any community gathering—the math says these struggles are in the room with you, even if nobody's talking about them.

This condition did not appear suddenly. It developed over centuries of systemic racism that taught African American communities to distrust institutions that claimed to offer help while delivering harm. Everything you learned in Chapter 2—the Tuskegee Study, medical experimentation, maternal mortality disparities—that's not ancient history. That's the foundation of why these numbers look the way they do today.

Trauma from slavery, segregation, and institutional abuse left marks that continue to influence behavior, belief, and survival strategies. Generational trauma from those eras shaped how help is perceived. Many learned through experience that systems designed to protect often caused damage instead. That history remains active rather than distant.

Growing up with the knowledge that ancestors were treated as property, punished for literacy, separated from family, and denied humanity changes how trust develops. Being asked to rely on a mental health system built without African American safety in mind creates understandable resistance.

That system has a documented history of misdiagnosis, racial bias, and unethical experimentation.

Jim Crow, segregation, redlining, mass incarceration, and repeated exposure to police violence reinforced that mistrust. These forces disrupted families, erased wealth, and created ongoing fear. Researchers describe this as intergenerational trauma, but the experience itself remains lived rather than theoretical. That trauma exists within bodies and nervous systems. It shapes responses to threat, authority, and vulnerability. It influences decisions about seeking care. Understanding the present requires recognizing how the past continues operating beneath the surface.

Let's talk about the elephant in the room: cost.

Economic pressure shapes mental health access at every level. Poverty, unemployment, and limited healthcare coverage turn treatment into an unreachable option. When survival requires constant calculation, therapy and medication fall outside the realm of possibility.

Here's what this looks like in practice: The average cost of therapy sessions ranges from $100 to $200 per session without insurance. Most therapists recommend weekly sessions, especially when starting treatment. Do the math: $100 per week = $400 per month = $4,800 per year. For a family living paycheck to paycheck, that's rent.

That's groceries. That's keeping the lights on.

Many African Americans juggle multiple jobs, overdue bills, family needs, and unreliable transportation. In that context, the suggestion to spend hundreds of dollars per month on therapy creates immediate conflict. Even with insurance, copays accumulate. A $30 copay per session still adds up to $120 per month, $1,440 per year. Without coverage, access disappears entirely.

The insurance gap is real and measurable: In 2020, 10.4% of Black adults in the U.S. had no form of health insurance (NAMI, 2025). That's more than 1 in 10 people. If you're at a family gathering of 30 people, 3 of them probably have zero access to insurance based mental health care. None. They're one crisis away from having nowhere to turn.

Race and economic status intersect in ways that deepen barriers. African Americans experience higher rates of underemployment and lower access to adequate insurance. These conditions directly restrict mental health care.

The effect remains consistent and measurable.

But even having insurance doesn't guarantee access. Mental health parity laws exist but lack enforcement. Insurers restrict access through administrative hurdles and low reimbursement rates. Coverage exists on paper while access collapses in reality: - Need pre-authorization? That's a barrier.

- Provider doesn't take your insurance? That's a barrier.

- Can't get time off work for appointments during business hours? That's a barrier.

- Closest in-network provider is 50 miles away? That's a barrier.

- No public transportation to get there? That's a barrier.

Missed work, long travel times, limited appointment availability, and transportation challenges push care further out of reach. Mental health services exist in theory, but remain inaccessible in practice.

And here's the cruel cycle: Untreated mental illness increases the risk of job loss, which then eliminates insurance, which makes treatment even less accessible. It's a downward spiral where the people who most need help are least able to access it.

Stigma is a barrier as real as any locked door. In many communities, mental health is still seen as something to be ashamed of. A weakness. A failure. Something you don't talk about, and you certainly don't seek help for.

It's like there's this invisible wall that stops people from talking about their struggles and getting the help they need. This wall is built from generations of messages: - "Be strong"

- "Don't show weakness"

- "Don't air your dirty laundry"

- "Keep your business to yourself"

- "Pull yourself up by your bootstraps"

- "Pray harder"

- "Just get over it"

These messages come from family. From church. From community. Often from places of love, from people who genuinely believe they're helping.

They're not trying to harm. They're repeating what they were taught, what helped them survive impossible circumstances.

But here's the hard truth: Survival strategies that worked in one context can become barriers in another. The stoicism and strength that helped our ancestors endure slavery and Jim Crow can make it harder for us to acknowledge when we're struggling and need help. The emphasis on keeping family business private, which protected Black families from systems that could use vulnerability against them, now keeps people suffering in silence.

The stigma operates on multiple levels: 1. Fear of being seen as weak within your own community. When strength has been necessary for survival for generations, admitting struggle feels like failing your ancestors.

2. Fear of confirming racist stereotypes about Black mental health.

There's a historical legacy of Black people being pathologized, labeled as naturally aggressive or unstable. Seeking mental health treatment can feel like playing into those narratives.

3. Fear that seeking help will be used against you. In custody battles.

In employment decisions. In interactions with systems like child protective services. These fears aren't paranoid—they're based on real experiences and real consequences.

Let me give you specific numbers on stigma's impact: Among Black adults who thought they needed mental health care but didn't try to find a provider, 30% said the main reason was they were afraid or embarrassed to seek care— compared to 18% of white adults (KFF, 2023).

Think about what that means: Nearly 1 in 3 Black adults who know they need help choose to suffer in silence because of shame. Because of embarrassment. Because the stigma feels more dangerous than the illness.

There's also a massive shortage of mental health professionals who understand the cultural nuances and specific needs of African Americans.

Only 4% of psychologists in the United States are Black, while Black Americans make up 13% of the population (University of Michigan School of Public Health, 2024). Only 2% of psychiatrists are Black (NAACP, 2025).

Let me put that in perspective: If you walk into a room with 100 psychologists, only 4 of them will be Black.

If you're looking specifically for a psychiatrist (a medical doctor who can prescribe medication), only 2 out of 100 will be Black.

Why does this gap matter so much?

It's hard to open up to someone who doesn't get where you're coming from.

Imagine trying to explain your experiences to someone who's never lived them. Trying to make someone understand how racism affects your daily life when they've never experienced it. Trying to describe the weight of generational trauma to someone whose ancestors weren't enslaved.

Having to educate your therapist about your reality uses up session time and emotional energy that should be going toward healing. It's exhausting.

It's invalidating. And for many people, it's a deal-breaker.

The research backs this up: Among adults who received or tried to receive mental health care, 46% of Black adults reported difficulty finding a provider who could understand their background and experiences—compared to 38% of white adults (KFF, 2023).

Breaking that down: Nearly half of Black Americans seeking mental health care struggle to find someone who gets them. Not half struggle to afford it (though many do). Not half struggle to schedule appointments (though many do). Half struggle to find someone who can understand their lived experience. That's a barrier that exists before treatment even begins.

And there's the licensure barrier making this worse: A 2022 report found that 84% of white people who took the licensed clinical social worker exam passed on their first try. For Black applicants? Just 45% passed on their first try, and only 57% of Black applicants ever passed the test (PBS, 2024).

Let me be clear about what this means: The gatekeeping mechanisms to become a licensed mental health professional are systematically screening out Black providers. Tests that white applicants pass at an 84% rate, Black applicants pass at a 45% rate. That's not measuring competence—that's measuring bias baked into the testing system.

This creates a feedback loop: Fewer Black providers → Harder for Black patients to find culturally competent care → More Black patients give up on treatment → Mental health disparities widen.

We also need to talk about how different identities within the Black community face different barriers.

Being Black in America creates specific mental health challenges. But being a Black woman adds gender-specific trauma. Being a Black LGBTQ person adds another layer of marginalization. Being a Black person with a disability adds yet another barrier. Being an elder has different implications than being a teenager.

Black women face compounding stress: - Higher rates of being single mothers (economic stress + parenting stress) - Maternal mortality crisis (medical trauma + fear for their lives during childbirth) - "Strong Black woman" stereotype that denies them the right to be vulnerable - Wage gap (earning 63 cents for every dollar white men earn) - Higher rates of sexual violence and domestic abuse Black LGBTQ individuals face: - Rejection from family and religious communities - Discrimination within both the Black community and LGBTQ spaces - Higher rates of homelessness, especially among youth - Violence and harassment - Struggle to find mental health providers who are both culturally competent around race AND knowledgeable about LGBTQ issues Black youth face: - School-to-prison pipeline - Over-disciplining and criminalization of normal childhood behavior - Lack of school counselors (many predominantly Black schools have no mental health resources) - Suicide rates that have been increasing dramatically (58% increase between 2011-2021 for Black Americans aged 15-24) Black elders face: - Lifelong accumulation of racial trauma - Higher rates of dementia and Alzheimer's - Social isolation - Fixed incomes that can't accommodate therapy costs - Generational stigma that's even stronger than among younger cohorts We need to recognize these layers and create support systems that actually work for everyone. Not one-size-fits-all programs that ignore diversity within African American communities. Not programs designed for white clients with African American faces added as an afterthought. Programs designed from the ground up to address intersecting identities and compounding barriers.

Culture can be both a strength and a barrier. The resilience and community bonds in African American culture are powerful. They've allowed us to survive and even thrive despite centuries of attempts to destroy us: - The emphasis on family and extended kinship networks - The role of the church as community anchor - The tradition of mutual aid and collective care - The creativity and joy we've created in the midst of suffering—through music, art, literature, dance - The spiritual practices that sustain us These are real strengths that support mental health and well-being. They're resources that culturally competent mental health care should build on, not ignore or pathologize.

But there's also this expectation to keep a stiff upper lip and not show weakness. To be strong no matter what. To endure. To keep going.

To not burden others with your problems. It's like carrying around a heavy backpack of unspoken rules and expectations.

This expectation comes from survival. During slavery, showing weakness could literally get you killed. During Jim Crow, appearing too "uppity" or "emotional" could invite violence. Even today, African Americans who express emotions in white spaces risk being seen as dangerous or unprofessional. So we learned to suppress our emotions and code-switch, saving our authentic selves for safe spaces.

And look, I get it. What kept us alive back then can hurt us now. The same strength that got us through impossible circumstances can make it hard to admit when we're struggling. That same privacy that protected us can isolate us. The resilience we celebrate can become a burden when it's expected at all times.

There's also the "Pandora's box" fear. The worry that if you start talking about mental health, everything will come flooding out and overwhelm you.

Better to keep the lid on, keep pushing through, keep maintaining the facade. This fear is particularly strong in communities that have experienced collective trauma. If everyone starts processing their pain at once, what happens? Will the community fall apart? Will we lose the strength that's held us together?

Faith communities can be complicated too. The Black church has been a source of incredible strength, community, and resistance. It's provided spiritual support, practical assistance, and political organizing. For many African Americans, faith is central to mental health and wellness. Prayer, worship, and spiritual community are legitimate sources of healing.

But some churches have also contributed to mental health stigma by preaching messages that: - Mental illness is a spiritual failing - Depression means you don't have enough faith - Medication is replacing God - Therapy is for weak people who aren't praying hard enough These messages, however well-intentioned, keep people from seeking the help they desperately need.

Breaking down these stigmas requires a both/and approach: You can have faith AND take medication. You can pray AND go to therapy. You can honor resilience without demanding it at all times. You can respect privacy while creating spaces for vulnerability. You can value cultural strength while challenging harmful aspects.

The current state of mental health in the African American community is a tangled web of data, obstacles, and cultural influences. But we can't just sit back and accept this. These are not just numbers. They're people.

When we say African Americans are 20% more likely to face mental health challenges, we're talking about: - Your cousin who can't get out of bed - Your coworker who flinches at sirens - Your friend who can't sleep because of nightmares - Your parent whose hands shake with anxiety - Your sibling who uses substances to numb pain they can't name - Your child who's acting out because they're terrified When we say

40% less likely to seek help, we're talking about those same people: - Suffering in silence - Going to work with depression - Raising kids while battling PTSD - Trying to hold relationships together while anxiety tears them apart - Functioning on the edge of crisis because they don't think help is available or accessible or for them These statistics reflect systemic issues that have been ignored for far too long. They're not natural. They're not inevitable. They're the predictable result of deliberate policy choices and systemic neglect: - The underinvestment in community mental health centers - The criminalization of mental illness - The lack of culturally competent care - The barriers insurance companies create - The stigma society maintains - The medical racism we documented in Chapter 2 All of it is by design or by neglect, and all of it is changeable.

Now you understand the numbers. You know that more Black Americans are struggling and fewer are getting help. You understand the barriers— economic, cultural, systemic. You've seen how stigma works, how the provider shortage matters, how insurance gaps create impossible choices.

But there's another barrier we haven't fully addressed yet, and it's literally life-threatening: What happens when you do reach out for help during a mental health crisis?

What happens when a family member calls 911 because someone they love is experiencing a psychiatric emergency?

In Chapter 4, we're going to confront the brutal reality that in African American communities, calling for help during a mental health crisis can be a death sentence. We're going to look at why police response to mental health emergencies is so deadly, particularly for Black Americans. We're going to examine the specific cases—Elijah McClain, Daniel Prude, Deborah Danner, Walter Wallace Jr., Michelle Cusseaux—and understand what systemic failures killed them.

Here's what you need to be prepared for: People with untreated mental illness are 16 times more likely to be killed by law enforcement than those without mental health challenges. In one out of every four police shootings, the person killed was experiencing a mental health crisis. For African Americans with mental illness, the risk multiplies even further.

We've seen the historical foundation in Chapter 2. We've examined the current crisis in Chapter 3. Now we need to confront the fact that the very act of seeking help—calling 911 during a psychiatric emergency—can turn a mental health crisis into a death sentence.

The barriers aren't just economic, cultural, and systemic. Sometimes the barrier is that seeking help gets you killed.

Chapter 4 is going to be hard. The stories are devastating. The patterns are infuriating. But you need to see it. You need to understand exactly how broken the system is. Because only when we face the full scope of the crisis can we fight for the change that's desperately needed.

You're ready. You've built the foundation. Let's keep going.

CHAPTER 4

You've seen the numbers in Chapter 3. You understand that African Americans are 20% more likely to face mental health challenges but 40% less likely to seek help. You know about the economic barriers, the stigma, the provider shortage. You've watched the statistics translate into real people in your life.

But there's one barrier we haven't fully confronted yet, and it's the most terrifying of all: Sometimes the act of calling for help during a mental health crisis becomes the thing that kills you.

In Chapter 1, you met Deborah Danner, Walter Wallace Jr., and Kayla Moore. Three people experiencing psychiatric emergencies. Three families who called 911 asking for help. Three deaths that never should have happened. You saw their stories. You felt their humanity. You understood their families' grief.

Now we need to examine the system that killed them.

This chapter isn't about retelling those individual tragedies—you already know their names, their ages, what they were holding when police shot them. This chapter is about understanding why police response to mental health crises is fundamentally broken, particularly in African

American communities. About examining the training gaps, the cultural failures, the policy choices that turn medical emergencies into death sentences. About looking at community trauma and the impossible calculations families make every single day.

This is about the system. The policies. The training. The funding. The choices people in power made that cost Deborah, Walter, and Kayla their lives.

And about what needs to change. Right now.

In African American communities, calling 911 during a mental health crisis is like playing Russian roulette with someone's life. You're supposed to get medical care and help. Instead, you get armed officers trained to respond to crime, rather than illness. Officers who see threat before they see sickness.

Officers who reach for their guns before they reach for understanding.

Let's be clear about the scope of this crisis with 2024-2025 data: People with untreated mental illness are 16 times more likely to be killed by law enforcement than those without mental health challenges. Sixteen times. Read that again.

In 2024—the highest year for deadly police encounters in 11 years—when information was available about the victim's mental state (70% of cases), 1 in 5 people killed by police exhibited signs of mental illness (Axios, 2025).

Nearly 25% of all fatal police encounters follow a response to disruptive behavior tied to an individual's mental health state or substance use disorder (Brookings, 2024). One out of every four police shootings involves someone in mental health crisis.

For African Americans with mental illness, the risk multiplies even further.

In Chicago, Black residents were more than 30 times more likely to be killed by police than white residents. In St. Louis, Black residents were more than 10 times more likely (Axios, 2025).

Let me translate those statistics into something you can feel: If you have 100 encounters between police and people experiencing mental health crises, 25 of them end in someone being killed. If those encounters involve Black Americans? The death rate climbs even higher. This isn't healthcare. This is systematic execution of people who are sick and need help.

The very act of seeking help—calling 911 during a psychiatric emergency— can be a death sentence. Families face an impossible choice every single day: watch their loved one suffer in silence, or call for help and risk police violence.

What kind of healthcare system is that? What kind of society forces people to make that calculation?

You want to know why this keeps happening? The answer is simple and infuriating.

Police officers receive an average of 130 hours of firearms training.

One hundred and thirty hours learning how to shoot. How to handle different weapons. How to hit targets under stress. How to reload. How to maintain weapons. How to use force.

But only 8 hours of crisis intervention training. And that's if they receive any mental health training at all. Many officers don't even get that.

Do the math with me: 130 hours learning to kill vs. 8 hours learning to deescalate. What message does that send about priorities? About what police departments value? About what they're preparing officers to do?

They're taught to establish control. Assert dominance. Use force when commands aren't followed. That's the playbook. That's what they know and that's what they do.

But here's the fundamental problem: A person experiencing psychosis can't just calm down on command. Someone in a manic episode can't simply stop resisting. A teenager with autism might not make eye contact or respond to verbal instructions the way officers expect. An elderly woman with schizophrenia might not drop scissors when ordered.

These are obvious symptoms of medical conditions. People who are sick and need help. But officers trained primarily in force application see noncompliance as a threat. They see mental health symptoms as resistance.

They see medical emergencies as criminal behavior.

The result? Escalation instead of de-escalation. Violence instead of care.

Death instead of treatment. Every single time.

Think back to the stories you read in Chapter 1: Deborah Danner wrote an essay predicting her own death at the hands of police responding to a mental health crisis. She knew the system was broken. She knew calling for help might mean death. A sergeant with crisis intervention training still shot and killed this 66-year-old woman holding scissors in her own bedroom.

Walter Wallace Jr.'s mother begged officers not to shoot her son. She explicitly told them he had mental health issues and was off his medication.

Officers had already been to the house three times that day without incident. Despite her pleas, despite the distance, despite having tasers available, two officers fired 14 shots. Walter died on the street in front of his family.

Kayla Moore was already restrained on a stretcher when police shot her nine times. Nine times. While EMS was trying to sedate her for transport to a hospital. While medical professionals were actively trying to help her. She died in the ambulance.

Now look at the pattern: - Families calling for help → Police arriving instead of mental health professionals - Officers using force → Instead of de-escalation techniques - People dying → Instead of receiving treatment - Families getting settlements → But no justice, no accountability - Officers rarely facing consequences → System continuing unchanged - Pattern repeating → Over and over and over This is what police response to mental health crises looks like in African American communities. This is why families hesitate to call 911. This is why people suffer in silence.

Every family with a loved one experiencing mental illness faces this calculation. Every single one.

Is the risk of calling 911 greater than the risk of not calling?

If your son is experiencing psychosis, threatening to harm himself, and you can't calm him down—do you call for help knowing police might kill him?

If your daughter with bipolar disorder is having a severe manic episode and could hurt herself—do you call 911 knowing she might end up dead instead of in treatment?

If your elderly mother with schizophrenia is having a crisis in her apartment —do you risk bringing armed officers into the situation knowing they might see her as a threat?

If your brother is having a breakdown and you're scared—do you call for help knowing the "help" that arrives will be carrying guns and trained to use force?

These shouldn't be choices families have to make. But in America, in Black American communities especially, these are daily realities. These are the calculations we make while our loved ones are suffering. While they need help. While we're terrified and desperate and out of options.

Think about what this means for the mental health crisis we documented in Chapters 2 and 3: We already established that African Americans are less likely to seek mental health treatment due to stigma, cost, provider shortage, and historical trauma. Now add this layer: Even when families overcome all those barriers and decide to seek help during a crisis, calling 911 might get their loved one killed.

The very system designed to help becomes an additional barrier to accessing care. The fear isn't irrational—it's based on documented patterns of police violence. The hesitation to call 911 isn't paranoia—it's pattern recognition and survival instinct.

Police departments love to point to Crisis Intervention Training (CIT) as the solution to this problem. Forty hours of training that teaches officers to recognize signs of mental illness, use de-escalation techniques, and connect people to services rather than jail.

It's better than nothing. Barely. But CIT has fundamental limitations that nobody wants to talk about.

First: It's optional. In most jurisdictions, CIT is voluntary. Even in cities that offer robust CIT programs, often fewer than 25% of officers complete it. Twenty-five percent. That means three out of four officers responding to mental health crises have zero specialized training.

Think about what that means when you call 911. You're rolling the dice hoping you get one of the quarter of officers who has any training at all in mental health response. And even if you do...

Second: It's inadequate. Forty hours of training cannot transform someone trained to use force into a mental health professional. You can't undo years of warrior cop mentality with a weeklong course. It doesn't work that way.

Consider this: To become a licensed social worker requires a master's degree (2-3 years of graduate education) plus 3,000+ hours of supervised clinical experience. To become a crisis counselor requires extensive education and training in psychology, de-escalation, trauma-informed care, cultural competency.

But we expect 40 hours of training to prepare police officers—who are fundamentally trained in control and force application—to handle the most volatile psychiatric emergencies? The math doesn't add up.

Third: It doesn't address the fundamental problem. The fundamental problem isn't that police lack training. It's that police are responding to medical emergencies in the first place. We're sending the wrong people.

Period.

When someone has a heart attack, we send paramedics. When someone has a stroke, we send EMTs. When someone has a broken bone, we send medical professionals. But when someone has a psychiatric emergency—a medical crisis involving the brain—we send armed officers trained in force application?

That's not a training problem. That's a system design problem.

Fourth: Police culture undermines it. Police culture emphasizes control, officer safety, and rapid resolution. Officers who use CIT techniques report being mocked by colleagues for taking too long. Being criticized by supervisors for being too soft. For not establishing control quickly enough.

For "babysitting" instead of "handling the situation."

The cultural message is clear: Using mental health skills makes you weak.

Taking time to de-escalate makes you ineffective. Treating people with psychiatric emergencies like patients instead of suspects makes you a liability.

CIT is a band-aid on a bullet wound. It doesn't address the core problem: we're sending the wrong people to respond to mental health crises. And people are dying because of it.

There's a better way. We know what works because we've seen it work.

In Eugene, Oregon. In Denver, Colorado. In cities around the world. The solution exists. The data exists. The proof exists.

The solution is mobile crisis response teams: mental health professionals, not police, responding to psychiatric emergencies.

For over 30 years, the Crisis Assistance Helping Out On The Streets (CAHOOTS) program has proven that alternative crisis response works.

Thirty years. This isn't experimental. This isn't theoretical. This is proven, tested, documented.

Team composition: - Medics (typically EMTs or paramedics) - Crisis workers (often with lived experience of mental health challenges) - NO police unless specifically requested Results from recent years: - Handle approximately 20% of all Eugene's 911 calls - Requested police backup on less than 1% of calls - Cost: $2.1 million annually - Savings: $8.5 million in avoided ambulance and ER costs - Deaths: Zero - Arrests: Zero Read that again. Zero deaths. Zero arrests. In tens of thousands of crisis responses over three decades.

What does this mean in human terms? Every person who had a CAHOOTS team respond to their crisis got help instead of handcuffs. Got treatment instead of trauma. Got connected to services instead of criminal records. Got to live.

Deborah Danner would be alive. Walter Wallace Jr. would be alive. Kayla Moore would be alive. If Eugene, Oregon's system had been in place in New York, Philadelphia, and Berkeley County, those families would still have their loved ones.

The Support Team Assisted Response (STAR) program launched in Denver in June 2020, directly responding to demands from Black Lives Matter protests. The community demanded alternatives to police response. Denver listened. They created STAR.

Results from recent evaluations: - Thousands of calls responded to - Zero arrests - Zero police backup requests -

33% reduction in crime in the service area (Yes, crime went DOWN when they sent mental health professionals instead of police) - Saved the city an estimated $20,000 per call compared to police and ambulance response This is what happens when cities prioritize solutions over punishment: Crime decreases. Costs decrease. People get help instead of criminal records. Communities heal instead of fracture.

It works. We know it works. We have years of data proving it works.

So why isn't every city doing this?

Here's the truth nobody wants to say out loud: We have the money. We just choose to spend it on the wrong things.

Police departments across America have received billions in military equipment through the Pentagon's 1033 program: armored vehicles, assault rifles, grenade launchers, aircraft. Money always seems available for weapons and military gear.

But when it comes to funding mobile crisis teams? Suddenly there's no budget. Suddenly it's too expensive. Suddenly we need to "study it more"and "consider the costs" and "wait for better economic conditions."

Let me break down the actual costs: CAHOOTS in Eugene costs $2.1 million annually and saves $8.5 million.

That's a net savings of $6.4 million per year. It doesn't cost money—it SAVES money while also saving lives.

STAR in Denver saves an estimated $20,000 per call compared to police response. Multiply that by thousands of calls. Do the math. The program pays for itself while preventing deaths.

Compare that to the costs of the current system: - Wrongful death settlements to families: Millions per case - Legal costs defending officers: Millions per case - Incarceration of people with mental illness who should be in treatment: $31,000-$60,000 per person per year - Emergency room visits that could be prevented: $1,000-$3,000 per visit - Long-term costs of untreated mental illness: Immeasurable We're spending more money on a system that kills people than it would cost to implement a system that saves lives and saves money.

This isn't about affordability. This is about priorities. This is about political will. This is about whether Black lives matter enough to fund the solutions that work.

When police kill someone during a mental health crisis, the trauma doesn't stop with that one death. It radiates outward like a shockwave through entire communities.

The ripple effects include: For families who witnessed the killing: - PTSD from watching their loved one die - Guilt from calling 911 ("I called for help and got them killed") - Grief compounded by trauma - Fear of ever calling for help again - Children traumatized by witnessing police violence For neighbors and community members: - Fear of calling 911 during crises - Increased anxiety and hypervigilance - Loss of trust in emergency response systems - Community-wide PTSD in neighborhoods with multiple police killings - Children learning that calling for help can be fatal For other people with mental illness in the community: - Increased reluctance to seek treatment - Fear of having police called during a crisis - Isolation from avoiding situations where someone might call 911 - Worsening symptoms due to fear and stress - Higher risk of suicide due to lack of intervention options For Black communities specifically: Research shows that police killings of unarmed Black Americans have spillover effects on the mental health of Black people who weren't directly involved. A 2018 study in The Lancet found that each police killing of an unarmed Black American was associated with worsening mental health among Black Americans in the general population (Bor et al., 2018).

Think about what this means: When Walter Wallace Jr. was killed in Philadelphia, it didn't just traumatize his family. It affected every Black person in Philadelphia who heard about it. Every Black parent who thought "that could have been my son." Every Black person with a family member who has mental illness. Every Black person who now has to recalculate the risks of calling 911.

The trauma compounds. Each new police killing adds to the cumulative trauma load Black communities carry. Each video shared on social media spreads the trauma wider. Each hashtag represents not just one death but thousands of people re-traumatized by witnessing violence against people who look like them.

The crisis of police violence during mental health encounters is not accidental. It's not a series of unfortunate incidents. It's the predictable result of deliberate policy choices spanning decades.

In the 1960s and 70s, America began closing psychiatric hospitals. This happened for good reasons—many state institutions were horrific places where people were abused, neglected, forgotten. Closing them was the right call.

The promise that accompanied closing these hospitals: Robust community mental health services would replace them. Outpatient clinics.

Crisis centers. Supportive housing. All the infrastructure needed to care for people in the community rather than institutions.

The reality: That promise never materialized. The funding never came. The infrastructure was never built.

The numbers tell the story: - In 1955: State psychiatric hospitals housed 559,000 people - Today: They house fewer than 38,000 - That's a 96% reduction in hospital beds - Community alternatives got about 20% of the funding they needed Where did those people go? Many ended up homeless. Many died on the streets. Many ended up in jails and prisons, which became America's new psychiatric institutions.

We didn't solve the problem. We just moved it. Made it worse. Made it more punitive.

Today, the three largest mental health facilities in America are jails: 1. Los Angeles County Jail 2. Cook County Jail (Chicago) 3. Rikers Island (New York) The largest mental health facilities in the richest country in the world are jails. Not hospitals. Not treatment centers. Jails.

Approximately 2 million people with mental illness are booked into jails annually. More than half of all incarcerated people have mental health problems. Half.

We didn't solve the problem of inadequate psychiatric care. We just moved it from hospitals to jails and made it worse in the process. We criminalized mental illness. We turned medical conditions into crimes and decided that punishment was easier than treatment.

In July 2022, the U.S. launched 988 as a national suicide and crisis hotline, modeled after 911. It was supposed to route people to mental health help instead of police. Great idea, right?

Except the federal government launched 988 without funding the infrastructure to support it.

Many 988 calls still result in police dispatch. Crisis centers that receive calls don't have mobile teams to send. Some states didn't allocate any funding for implementation. The system was set up to fail.

And Black communities pay the price. Again.

We know what needs to happen. The solutions exist. What's missing is political will. People in power deciding that Black lives matter enough to actually fund the solutions.

Here's what must happen: 1. Community-Based Crisis Response in Every City - Mobile crisis teams staffed by mental health professionals - 24/7 availability - No police involvement unless requested for safety - Culturally competent teams that reflect community demographics - Funded at levels that allow adequate staffing and rapid response 2. Eliminate Police as First Responders to Mental Health Crises - Dispatch mental health teams, not police, to psychiatric emergencies - Police backup only when explicitly requested - Train 911 dispatchers to screen calls and route appropriately - Change default response from armed force to medical care 3. Mandatory and Robust Training for ANY Police Who Respond - Not 8 hours. Not 40 hours. Ongoing, continuous training - Focus on de-escalation, not control - Cultural competency training specific to Black communities - Understanding of how racism and trauma affect mental health - Accountability for officers who fail to use de-escalation 4. Fully Fund Community Mental Health Infrastructure - Outpatient clinics in every neighborhood - Crisis stabilization centers as alternatives to jails - Supportive housing for people with serious mental illness - Peer support programs staffed by people with lived experience - Funding that matches the need, not political convenience 5. Medicaid Expansion and Mental Health Parity Enforcement - Every state must expand Medicaid - Enforce existing mental health parity laws - Increase reimbursement rates so providers can afford to accept Medicaid - Make insurance coverage meaningful, not theoretical 6. Community Accountability and Oversight - Community review boards with real power - Transparent data collection on police use of force - Mandatory reporting of all mental health-related police encounters - Consequences for departments that fail to implement alternatives You've now seen the full scope of the mental health crisis in African American communities: Chapter 1: The human faces—Deborah, Walter, Kayla—people who should be alive Chapter 2: The historical foundation— slavery, medical racism, generational trauma Chapter 3: The current barriers—economics, stigma, provider shortage Chapter 4: The deadly system—police response failures, training gaps, government inaction You understand why the numbers are what they are. You know why families hesitate to call for help. You've seen how the very systems designed to help can become instruments of harm.

Now comes the hardest and most important part: What do we do about it?

Chapter 5 will give you concrete, actionable solutions. Not vague calls for "awareness" or "conversation." Real strategies for: - Finding culturally competent mental health care - Navigating the system when resources are limited - Supporting family members in crisis - Building community-based solutions - Advocating for systemic change - Protecting yourself and your loved ones You've built the foundation of understanding. Now we build the path forward.

The situation is dire, but it's not hopeless. Solutions exist. Programs work.

Lives can be saved. But only if we stop accepting the status quo. Only if we demand better. Only if we fight for the change that communities desperately need.

Are you ready to move from understanding to action? Let's go.

Axios. (2025, February 25). New data shows 2024 was highest year for deadly police encounters in 11 years. Retrieved from https://www.axios.com/2025/02/25/police-shooting-violence-black-latino2024 Brookings Institution. (2024, July 30). A crisis within a crisis: Police killings of Black emerging adults. Retrieved from https://www.brookings.edu/articles/a-crisis-within-a-crisis-police-killings-ofblack-emerging-adults/ Mapping Police Violence. (2025). 2025 Police Violence Report. Retrieved from https://policeviolencereport.org/ Mapping Police Violence. (2024). 2024 Police Violence Report. Retrieved from https://policeviolencereport.org/2024/ Bor, J., Venkataramani, A. S., Williams, D. R., & Tsai, A. C. (2018). Police killings and their spillover effects on the mental health of Black Americans: A population-based, quasi-experimental study. The Lancet, 392(10144), 302310.

Massachusetts General Hospital Psychiatry News. (2023, February 9). How police violence takes a toll on the mental health of Black Americans.

Retrieved from https://mghpsychnews.org/quantifying-the-mental-healthimpact-of-police-killings-on-black-americans/ Psychiatric Services. (2021). Dying at the intersections: Police-involved killings of Black people with mental illness. Retrieved from https://psychiatryonline.org/doi/10.1176/appi.ps.20200094 2 Washington Post. (2022). Police shootings database 2015-2024: Search by race, age, department. Retrieved from https://www.washingtonpost.com/graphics/investigations/police-shootingsdatabase/ Community Solutions. (n.d.). The impact of policing on Black mental health.

Retrieved from https://www.communitysolutions.com/resources/impactpolicing-black-mental-health Penn Today. (n.d.). Police killings and Black mental health. University of Pennsylvania. Retrieved from https://penntoday.upenn.edu/news/policekillings-and-black-mental-health

CHAPTER 5

You've seen the full picture now. The historical trauma. The current barriers. The deadly police response failures. The government inaction. The funding gaps. You understand the system.

But understanding alone doesn't keep you alive. Understanding doesn't get you treatment. Understanding doesn't stop your depression or calm your anxiety or help you sleep at night when the trauma feels overwhelming.

This chapter is different. This chapter is about action.

Not vague encouragement to "raise awareness" or "start a conversation."

Concrete steps you can take today. Right now. Before you finish reading this chapter. Steps that work whether you have insurance or not. Whether you have money or not. Whether there's a Black therapist in your area or not.

Because here's the truth: The system is broken and needs to change.

That's Chapter 4's message, and it's absolutely real. But you can't wait for the system to fix itself before you take care of your mental health. You can't wait for police departments to fund mobile crisis teams before you address your anxiety. You can't wait for Medicaid expansion before you deal with your depression.

You need help now. This chapter shows you how to get it.

We're going to cover: - Finding culturally competent therapy when providers are scarce - Accessing care when money is tight - Protecting yourself during mental health crises - Supporting family members who are struggling - Building community-based support systems - Advocating for systemic change while taking care of yourself Let's get to work.

Cultural competency isn't just nice to have. It's essential for effective treatment.

When therapists lack cultural competency, they: - Miss symptoms because they don't recognize how Black Americans express mental health challenges - Misdiagnose conditions (Black men get misdiagnosed with schizophrenia when they actually have PTSD or mood disorders) - Don't understand how racism and discrimination affect mental health - Can't connect treatment to your lived experience - Make you feel misunderstood, judged, or invalidated Research shows that culturally competent therapy leads to: - Better treatment outcomes - Higher rates of completing treatment - Stronger therapeutic relationships - More accurate diagnoses - Treatment plans that actually work in your real life Don't wait until you're in the room to find out if a therapist gets it.

Most therapists offer free 15-minute phone consultations. Use them. Here are the questions to ask: About their experience: - "Have you treated other Black clients?"

- "Have you received training in cultural competence for Black mental health?"

- "Are you familiar with racial trauma and how to treat it?"

About their approach: - "How do you see our cultural backgrounds influencing our work together?"

- "Will you integrate my beliefs, practices, and cultural background into treatment?"

- "Do you use different approaches when working with patients from different cultural backgrounds?"

About their awareness: - "What is your current understanding of health disparities for Black patients?"

- "How do you handle discussions about racism and discrimination?"

- "Are you comfortable talking about police violence, systemic racism, and how they affect mental health?"

Pay attention to: - Do they welcome these questions or seem defensive?

- Do they acknowledge racism's impact on mental health?

- Do they seem open to learning or act like they know everything?

- Do they ask about your experiences or make assumptions?

Red flags: - "I don't see color" or "I treat everyone the same"

- Minimizing racism: "Everyone faces challenges"

- Getting defensive about questions - Claiming expertise without specific training or experience - Not acknowledging power dynamics Green flags: - Acknowledges limitations: "I haven't worked with many Black clients, but I'm committed to learning"

- Asks about your preferences and needs - Demonstrates humility and openness - Acknowledges racism's impact on mental health - Welcomes ongoing feedback about cultural issues Only 4% of psychologists and

2% of psychiatrists are Black. That's the reality. But there are specific directories and organizations focused on connecting Black people with culturally competent care: National Directories (FREE to search): 1. Therapy for Black Girls (therapyforblackgirls.com) - Directory of therapists committed to Black women's mental health - Filter by location, insurance, specialty, therapy type - Podcast and resources on mental health topics 2. Therapy for Black Men (therapyforblackmen.org) - Directory specifically for Black men seeking judgment-free care - Culturally competent therapists and coaches - All 50 states 3. Melanin & Mental Health (@melaninandmentalhealth) - Connects Black & Latinx/Hispanic communities with culturally competent clinicians - Monthly events and resources - Online directory 4. Black Mental Health Alliance (410-338-2642 | blackmentalhealth.com) - "Find a Therapist" locator - Information and resources - Evidence-based information from Black perspective 5. Inclusive Therapists (inclusivetherapists.com) - Broader directory with filters for race, LGBTQ+ identity, religion - Search specifically for therapists trained in racial trauma 6. BEAM (Black Emotional & Mental Health Collective) (beam.community) - Training, advocacy, and resources - Removing barriers to emotional health care - Grant-making organization supporting Black mental health initiatives Specialized Organizations: For Black Women: - Sista Afya Community

Mental Wellness - Sustains mental wellness of Black women through community building - The Loveland Foundation - Provides financial support for therapy for Black women and girls - Black Women's Health Imperative - Health equity and social justice advocacy For Black Men: - The Confess Project of America - Mental health support for Black boys, men, and families - My Brother's Keeper Cares - Support network within urban environment For Black Youth: - AAKOMA Project - Helps diverse teenagers and families achieve optimal mental health - The Steve Fund - Programs for mental health and well-being of young people of color For LGBTQ+ Black Individuals: - National Queer & Trans Therapists of Color Network (NQTTCN) Healing justice organization - Black LGBTQ+ affirming therapists through Inclusive Therapists directory Faith-Based Organizations: - Check if your church has mental health ministry or therapist partnerships - Some faith communities maintain lists of culturally competent providers who respect spiritual beliefs Real talk: In many areas, there simply aren't Black therapists available.

That's the reality of the 4% statistic. You still deserve treatment.

Non-Black therapists can provide effective, culturally competent care IF: - They've received training in cultural competency - They acknowledge racism's impact on mental health - They're open to learning about your experiences - They don't get defensive when you educate them - They integrate your cultural identity into treatment - They actively work to check their biases How to work with non-Black therapists effectively: Set expectations early: "I need you to understand that racism and discrimination are central to my mental health challenges. Can you work with that?"

Educate when you have energy, set boundaries when you don't: Some sessions, you might have energy to explain microaggressions or systemic racism. Other times, you need to focus on your immediate crisis.

Both are okay. You're the client, not the educator.

Give feedback: "When you said [X], it felt like you were minimizing my experience with racism."

"I need you to understand that this isn't 'just anxiety'—it's racial trauma."

Be willing to fire them: If they're not getting it after you've given feedback, find someone else. Your mental health is too important to waste time with a therapist who doesn't understand your reality.

Use session time strategically: You can spend some sessions processing racial trauma with guidance from a culturally aware (even if not Black) therapist and use community support groups for experiences only other Black people will fully understand.

1. Community Health Centers - Federally Qualified Health Centers (FQHCs) provide mental health services on sliding scale based on income - Some offer free care for uninsured patients - Find centers at: findahealthcenter.hrsa.gov 2. University Training Clinics - Graduate students in psychology/social work programs provide therapy supervised by licensed professionals - Significantly reduced rates ($5-$30 per session) - Search: "[Your city] university psychology clinic" or "counseling training clinic"

3. Open Path Collective (openpathcollective.org) - Therapists offering sessions for $30-$80 - One-time membership fee: $59 - Nationwide network 4. NAMI (National Alliance on Mental Illness) - Free support groups nationwide - Peer-led groups for specific conditions - Family support groups - Find local groups: nami.org 5. The Boris Lawrence Henson Foundation - Offers free virtual therapy sessions (limited availability) - Specifically for African Americans experiencing stress/trauma - Check website for current programs: borislhensonfoundation.org 6. The Loveland Foundation - Financial support for therapy for Black women and girls - Covers cost of sessions - Apply at: thelovelandfoundation.org 7. Therapy Apps with Free Tiers -

7 Cups: Free emotional support from trained listeners - Wysa: AI chatbot for mental health support (free basic version) - Shine: Mental health app specifically for people of color (free version available) 8. Crisis Services (Always Free) - 988 Suicide & Crisis Lifeline: Call or text 988 - Crisis Text Line: Text HOME to 741741 - Black Mental Health Hotline: Call or text 1-866-244-7470 - Trans Lifeline: (877) 565-8860 If you have Medicaid: - Many providers don't accept Medicaid because reimbursement rates are low - But some do. Call your state's Medicaid managed care plan and ask for their mental health provider directory - Ask specifically: "Which providers are accepting new Medicaid patients?"

- FQHCs are required to accept Medicaid If you have private insurance: - Check if your plan covers teletherapy (often more options than in-person) - Verify coverage BEFORE first appointment - Ask about: - Copay per session - Deductible requirements - Annual session limits - Out-of-network coverage (sometimes you can see non-covered therapists and get partial reimbursement) If you're uninsured: - Check if you qualify for Medicaid: healthcare.gov - Look into state-specific programs (some states offer mental health coverage even if you don't qualify for full Medicaid) - Ask therapists about sliding scale fees (many offer reduced rates based on income even if not advertised) Many therapists have flexibility they don't advertise. Ask: "Do you offer sliding scale fees based on income?"

"I can afford $X per session. Is there any way to make that work?"

"Do you have any pro bono slots available?"

"Can we do every other week instead of weekly to reduce costs?"

Some therapists will say yes. Some won't. But you won't know unless you ask.

When you're in crisis, you can't think clearly. That's why you plan now, when you're stable.

Your crisis plan should include: 1. Warning Signs (What tells you you're heading toward crisis?) Examples: - Sleeping more than 12 hours or less than 4 hours - Not eating for 24+ hours - Suicidal thoughts becoming more frequent/intense - Isolating for multiple days - Neglecting basic hygiene - [Your specific signs] 2. Coping Strategies (What helps you, even a little?) Examples: - Calling [specific person] - Going for a walk - Taking a shower - Listening to [specific music] - Petting your dog - [Your strategies] 3. People to Call (In order) 1. [Trusted friend/family member] - [Phone number] 2. [Therapist if you have one] - [Phone number] 3. [Crisis hotline] - 988 or 1-866-244-7470 (Black

Mental Health Hotline) 4. [Backup person] - [Phone number] 4. What NOT to Do - Do NOT call 911 unless you have exhausted all other options - If you must call 911, try to have an advocate with you who can tell dispatchers: "This is a mental health emergency. Send crisis team, not police."

- Do NOT go to ER alone if possible (bring advocate who can explain situation) 5. Information for Others - Diagnosis (if you have one) - Medications you're taking - Allergies - What helps when you're in crisis - What makes things worse Write this down. Share with trusted people. Keep a copy in your phone.

Remember Chapter 4: Calling 911 during a mental health crisis can be deadly for Black Americans. Here are alternatives: 1. Crisis Text/Phone Lines (Mental Health Professionals, Not Police) - 988 Suicide & Crisis Lifeline - Crisis Text Line: Text HOME to 741741 - Black Mental Health Hotline: 1-866-244-7470 - SAMHSA National Helpline: 1-800-662-4357 (treatment referral) 2. Mobile Crisis Teams (If Available in Your Area) - Search: "[Your city] mobile crisis team"

- These send mental health professionals instead of police - Available in limited areas but expanding - If available, save number in your crisis plan 3. Crisis Stabilization Centers - Walk-in centers for mental health crises - Alternative to ER - Search: "[Your city] crisis stabilization center"

- Not available everywhere, but worth checking 4. Telehealth Crisis Services - Some insurance plans offer 24/7 telehealth mental health crisis lines - Check your insurance card for "behavioral health crisis" number 5. Trusted Person Network - Build a network of people you can call before crisis escalates - Give them permission to check on you - Share your crisis plan with them Sometimes police get called despite your best efforts. A neighbor calls.

A well-meaning family member calls. You're in public and someone calls.

Here's how to reduce risk: If you're with the person in crisis: - Tell 911 dispatcher: "This is a mental health emergency"

- Ask for CIT-trained officers if available - Stay on scene if safe to do so - When officers arrive, immediately identify yourself and explain: - "This person is having a mental health crisis"

- "They are not violent"

- "They need medical help, not arrest"

- State their diagnosis if known - Mention any medications If you're the person in crisis and police arrive: - Keep hands visible at all times - Move slowly - Speak calmly even if you don't feel calm - Say: "I'm having a mental health emergency. I need medical help."

- Don't make sudden movements - If possible, ask for crisis intervention team or mental health professional - Ask for advocate/family member to be contacted This is unfair. This shouldn't be necessary. But it can save your life.

You can't force someone into treatment. But you can create conditions where they're more likely to accept help.

What helps: Express concern without judgment: "I've noticed you seem different lately. I'm worried about you. Can we talk?"

NOT: "What's wrong with you?" or "You need therapy."

Listen more than you talk: Let them share their experience without interrupting or offering immediate solutions.

Validate their feelings: "That sounds really hard" or "I can understand why you'd feel that way"

NOT: "It's not that bad" or "Other people have it worse"

Offer specific support: "Can I help you find a therapist?" or "Would it help if I went with you to the first appointment?"

NOT: "Let me know if you need anything" (too vague) Check in regularly but don't hover: Consistent, brief check-ins show you care without overwhelming them Take care of yourself: You can't pour from an empty cup. Supporting someone with mental illness is exhausting. Get your own support.

If they express suicidal thoughts: - Take it seriously ALWAYS - Ask directly: "Are you thinking about suicide?"

- Ask: "Do you have a plan?"

- If they have a plan, this is a crisis—get immediate help - Don't promise to keep suicidal plans secret - Remove means if possible (guns, pills, etc.) If they're a danger to themselves or others: - This is when you may need to call for help - Try crisis lines FIRST before 911 - If you must call 911, be explicit: "Mental health emergency, send CIT officers"

- Stay with them if safe If they're psychotic (seeing/hearing things that aren't there, severe paranoia): - Speak calmly and don't argue with delusions - Remove them from triggering environment if possible - Contact their doctor/therapist if they have one - This may require emergency intervention but try mobile crisis teams

FIRST

NAMI Family Support Groups (nami.org) - Free support groups specifically for families - Led by trained family members - Learn strategies from others in similar situations NAMI Family-to-Family - Free 8-week education program - Learn about diagnoses, treatment, coping strategies - Connect with other families Black Mental Wellness - Resources from Black perspective - Training opportunities - Community connection You can love someone and still have boundaries.

It's okay to: - Say "I can't talk right now, but I can call you tomorrow"

- Set limits on how often you provide crisis support - Ask them to call therapist/crisis line instead of you sometimes - Take a break when you're overwhelmed - Protect your own mental health Boundaries aren't punishment. They're preservation.

Tell your loved one: "I care about you AND I need to take care of myself so I can keep being here for you."

Individual therapy is important. But it's not enough.

African American healing traditions have always been communal. From the ring shout to church testimony, from kitchen table conversations to beauty shop therapy, we heal together.

Community support provides: - Shared understanding you don't have to explain - Validation from people with similar experiences - Practical help and resource sharing - Accountability and encouragement - Sense of belonging and connection - Cultural affirmation You need BOTH professional treatment AND community support.

Not either/or.

Existing Support Groups: NAMI Support Groups (nami.org) - Free peer-led support groups - Some specifically for African Americans - Groups for specific conditions (depression, bipolar, PTSD, anxiety) - Also groups for family members Black Mental Wellness Support Groups - Check local area for Black-specific mental health groups - Search: "[Your city] Black mental health support group"

Online Support Groups: - BEAM Community - Black Mental Health Matters Facebook groups - Reddit communities: r/BlackMentalHealth - Therapy for Black Girls online community Faith-Based Support: - Some churches have mental health ministries with support groups - Ask your pastor/church leader about mental health support Creating Your Own Support Circle: If formal groups don't exist in your area, create informal support: 1. Start Small (3-5 people) - Friends, family, coworkers who "get it"

- People you trust who also struggle with mental health - Meet monthly or weekly 2. Set Ground Rules - Confidentiality (what's said here stays here) - No judgment, no advice unless asked - Everyone gets time to share - No phones during meeting 3. Structure Meetings - Opening check-in (how is everyone?) - Sharing time (what's going on in your life?) - Resource sharing (what's helping you lately?) - Closing (words of encouragement) 4. Keep It Sustainable - Don't make it too formal or it becomes work - Rotate hosting if meeting in person - Use video chat if in-person is hard - It's okay to take breaks Traditional mutual aid in Black communities: - Sharing childcare - Meal trains when someone's struggling - Carpooling to appointments - Sharing information about resources - Financial support (passing the hat) - Skill sharing (haircuts, car repairs, tutoring in exchange for other services) Modern applications for mental health: Create a Shared Resource List: - Therapists who take Medicaid - Free/low-cost services in area - Crisis resources - Transportation options - Food assistance (because food security affects mental health) Practical Support Exchanges: - "I'll watch your kids so you can go to therapy"

- "I'll drive you to appointments"

- "I'll check in on you daily when you're struggling"

- "I'll cook extra and bring you meals"

Financial Cooperation: - Crowdfunding therapy costs for community members - Collective bargaining with therapists (group rates) - Sharing prescription discount resources This is how communities survive when systems fail.

Self-care isn't luxury. It's survival. But it has to be realistic for your life.

Morning Routine (10 minutes) - Wake up at consistent time (even weekends) - Breathe intentionally for 2 minutes (See breathing exercise below) - Drink water before coffee/phone - Move your body for 5 minutes (stretch, walk, dance) - Set one intention for the day Work/Day Protection - Take actual lunch break away from desk - Set boundaries on availability if possible - Notice when you're overwhelmed and take 5-minute breaks - Move every 2 hours (walk, stretch, bathroom break) Evening Wind-Down (30 minutes before bed) - No screens 30-60 minutes before bed - Dim lights - Journal for 5 minutes (dump thoughts on paper) - Breathing or meditation - Read something calming (not news) - Same bedtime every night Weekly - One activity just for joy (not productive, just enjoyable) - Connect with someone who fills your cup - Move your body intentionally for 30+ minutes - Cook a real meal (cooking can be meditative) - Rest without guilt This activates your parasympathetic nervous system (your body's calm-down system): 1. Sit comfortably, feet flat on floor 2. Place one hand on chest, one on belly 3. Breathe in through nose for 4 counts (belly expands) 4. Hold for 4 counts 5. Breathe out through mouth for 6 counts (make "whoosh" sound) 6. Pause for 2 counts 7. Repeat 5 times Use it: - Before difficult conversations - During panic attacks - When you can't sleep - After trauma/triggering events - When you feel rage building Do it now. Right now. Put the book down. Try one cycle.

Exercise isn't punishment. It's medicine.

What exercise does for your brain: - Releases endorphins (natural mood boosters) - Increases serotonin and dopamine (happiness chemicals) - Reduces cortisol (stress hormone) - Improves sleep - Gives sense of accomplishment - Gets you out of your head, into your body Find movement you actually enjoy: If you like being alone: Walking, jogging, home workout videos, yoga, swimming If you need community: Group fitness classes, sports teams, walking groups, dance classes If you have limited mobility: Chair yoga, water aerobics, gentle stretching, tai chi If you're on tight budget: Walking (free), YouTube workouts (free), dancing in living room (free), bodyweight exercises (free) If you love music: Put on a song and move however feels good Start with 10 minutes. Don't wait for perfect conditions. Walk today.

Poor sleep makes EVERYTHING worse. Depression, anxiety, concentration, physical health.

Sleep basics: - Same bedtime and wake time every day (yes, weekends too) - Room dark and cool (65-68 degrees) - No screens 1 hour before bed (blue light blocks melatonin) - No caffeine after 2 PM (stays in system 6-8 hours) - Wind-down routine (30 minutes of calm activity) - Use bed only for sleep (not work, TV, scrolling) If you try these for 2 weeks and still struggle, see a doctor. Sleep problems can signal depression, anxiety, or physical conditions needing treatment.

What you eat directly affects your mood. Your gut makes 90% of your body's serotonin.

Foods that help mental health: - Omega-3s: Salmon, sardines, walnuts, flaxseed (reduce depression) - Complex carbs: Whole grains, sweet potatoes, oats (stabilize mood) - Protein: Lean meats, beans, eggs (brain chemical building blocks) - Leafy greens: Spinach, kale, collards (folate for mood) - Fermented foods: Yogurt, kimchi, sauerkraut (gut health) Foods that hurt mental health: - Too much sugar (crashes and mood swings) - Highly processed foods (lack nutrients) - Excessive alcohol (depresses nervous system, disrupts sleep) - Too much caffeine (triggers anxiety) Balance is key. Soul food is culture and heritage. Mac and cheese, fried chicken, cornbread connect us to our roots. You can honor culture AND take care of your body. Both things can be true.

Loneliness is as harmful to health as smoking 15 cigarettes a day.

Your body treats loneliness like a physical threat.

When energy is low: - Text a friend - Join online support groups (watch until ready to talk) - Call/FaceTime while doing something else - Sit on porch where neighbors might pass When you have more energy: - Go to church/faith community events - Join book club, game night, hobby group - Volunteer (helping others helps us) - Take a class - Host small gathering (nothing fancy) - Join sports league or fitness class - Attend community events - Start support group Quality over quantity. One real friendship helps more than 100 followers.

Before therapy offices and prescription medications, our ancestors had sophisticated healing practices that kept them whole through unspeakable trauma.

These aren't replacements for modern mental health care. They work ALONGSIDE it.

In West African tradition, griots kept history alive and helped people process trauma through stories.

When you share your story: - You organize chaos into narrative - You create distance from overwhelming emotions - You connect to others with similar experiences - Your story becomes someone else's lifeline Ways to practice: - Journaling (10 minutes daily, stream-of-consciousness, no editing) - Voice memos (sometimes speaking is easier than writing) - Sharing with trusted people - Creative expression (poetry, music, art when words aren't enough) From work songs to gospel to modern dance, sound and movement have always been African American medicine.

Why it works: - Music therapy reduces anxiety and depression - Dancing releases trauma stored in body - Drumming synchronizes brain waves, creates connection - Singing releases endorphins, helps breathing Make healing playlists: - Sad songs when you need to cry - Uplifting songs when you need hope Sing: - In shower, car, church choir - Singing releases endorphins Dance alone: - Put on music, move however your body wants - Not about looking good— about releasing emotion trapped in muscles Make music: - Drumming, singing, playing instruments - No skill required

Our ancestors used healing plants. Modern science confirms what traditional healers knew.

Herbs that can help: - Chamomile: Reduces anxiety, improves sleep (tea) - Lavender: Calms nervous system (tea, essential oil, dried herb) - Peppermint: Eases stress-related stomach issues, improves focus - Lemon balm: Reduces anxiety, lifts mood - Ashwagandha: Helps body handle stress (adaptogen)

CRITICAL CAUTIONS:

- Natural ≠ safe - Herbs can interact with medications - Quality matters—buy from reputable sources - These ADD to necessary medications, don't replace them - If you're on psychiatric medications, talk to doctor before adding herbs In African cultures, mental health wasn't just individual problem. If someone struggled, community gathered.

Modern applications: - Work with neighbors to share resources, skills, childcare - Join/create mutual aid networks - Church mental health ministries (blending spiritual support with mental health awareness) - Support groups for Black folks facing similar challenges - Regular honest conversations where "I'm not okay" is safe Key: Creating spaces where vulnerability is safe, suffering isn't shameful, support is abundant.

For many African Americans, faith and church are central to wellbeing. The Black church has been strength through slavery, Jim Crow, Civil Rights.

But some religious communities: - Make mental illness seem like lack of faith - Suggest prayer can replace medication - Shame people for getting professional help - Use scripture to dismiss psychological suffering Truth: Faith and mental health care are NOT opposites. They work together beautifully.

You can: - Pray AND take medication - Trust God AND see therapist - Have strong faith AND struggle with depression Look for faith communities that: - Have mental health ministries - Partner with mental health professionals - Discuss mental health from pulpit - Make space for real struggle (not just victory testimonies) - See therapy and medication as God's provision Biblical figures struggled with mental health: - Elijah's depression after mountaintop experience - David's mood swings throughout Psalms - Job's trauma and suffering Taking care of the mind God gave you is stewardship, not weakness.

You can work on your personal mental health AND fight for systemic change. Not either/or.

Set boundaries on advocacy work: - Decide how much time/energy you can give - It's okay to say "I can't take this on right now"

- Protect yourself from vicarious trauma - Take breaks from news and social media Choose your lanes: - You don't have to fight every battle - Focus on issues most important to you - Work where your skills and passion align Practice sustainable activism: - Work in community, not alone - Celebrate small wins - Rest isn't weakness—it's strategy - Burnout helps no one Local Level: 1. Attend city council meetings - Speak during public comment about mental health funding - Demand mobile crisis teams instead of police response - Push for crisis stabilization centers 2. Contact local representatives - Email, call, or write about mental health priorities - Share your story (if you're comfortable) - Be specific about what you want (funding amounts, programs, etc.) 3. Join or create mental health advocacy groups - NAMI local affiliates - Black mental health advocacy organizations - Faith-based mental health ministries 4. Support organizations doing the work - BEAM (Black Emotional & Mental Health Collective) - Boris Lawrence Henson Foundation - Black Mental Health Alliance - The Confess Project - Volunteer or donate if you can State Level: 1. Medicaid Expansion - If your state hasn't expanded Medicaid, make noise about it - Contact state legislators - Support advocacy organizations pushing for expansion 2. Mental Health Parity Enforcement - Demand insurance companies follow mental health parity laws - File complaints when insurers deny coverage - Support legislation strengthening enforcement 3. School-Based Mental Health Services - Push for counselors in schools (current ratio: 1 counselor per 482 students) - Demand culturally competent services - Advocate for mental health education in curriculum National Level: 1. Vote for candidates who prioritize mental health - Research candidates' positions - Ask about mental health plans during town halls - Make mental health funding a deciding issue 2. Support federal legislation - Contact federal representatives about mental health bills - Sign petitions - Share information with networks 3. Share your story strategically - Op-eds in local papers - Social media campaigns - Testify at hearings - Speak at community events You don't have to do all of this. Pick ONE thing. Do it consistently.

That's advocacy.

988 Suicide & Crisis Lifeline - Call or text 988 - 24/7, free, confidential - Connects to crisis centers nationwide Black Mental Health Hotline - Call or text: 1-866-244-7470 - Culturally competent crisis support - Specifically for Black community Crisis Text Line - Text HOME to 741741 - 24/7, free, confidential - Text-based support SAMHSA National Helpline - 1-800-662-4357 - Treatment referral and

information - 24/7, free, confidential Trans Lifeline (for transgender individuals) - (877) 565-8860 - Run by and for trans people The Trevor Project (LGBTQ+ youth) - 1-866-488-7386 - Text START to 678-678 - 24/7 crisis support for LGBTQ+ young people If you're having suicidal thoughts RIGHT NOW: 1. Call/text crisis line immediately (988 or 1-866-244-7470) 2. Remove means (give someone guns, pills, anything you could use) 3. Don't be alone (call someone, go to public place) 4. Go to ER if necessary (bring advocate if possible) Tell yourself: "These feelings are temporary. I don't have to act on them. I can get through the next hour."

Make it through the next hour. Then the next. That's enough.

You've read about the system. You understand the barriers. You know the history. You see the injustice.

Now you have the tools: - How to find culturally competent therapy - How to access care when money is tight - How to protect yourself during crises - How to support family members - How to build community support - How to practice self-care that actually works - How to reclaim healing traditions - How to advocate for change The system is broken. But you're not broken. You deserve healing.

You deserve support. You deserve peace.

Take one action from this chapter. Just one. Today.

- Save crisis numbers in your phone - Search for therapist using one of the directories - Create your crisis plan - Text one person you trust - Try the breathing exercise - Join one support group - Take a 10-minute walk One action. That's how change starts. Not with perfect plans. With one step.

You don't have to fix everything. You don't have to heal overnight.

You don't have to wait until you can afford the perfect therapist. You can start where you are. With what you have. Right now.

The well is still running. Chapter by chapter, we've traced the stream from its poisoned source through the barriers blocking its flow.

We've seen the system that turns help into harm. And now you have tools to dig your own channels, to find water where the system says there is none.

Your healing matters. Your mental health matters. Your life matters.

Take care of yourself. Build community. Demand change. All three.

Not either/or.

The work continues. But you have what you need to begin.

- Therapy for Black Girls: therapyforblackgirls.com - Therapy for Black Men: therapyforblackmen.org - Melanin & Mental Health: @melaninandmentalhealth - Black Mental Health Alliance: (410) 338-2642 | blackmentalhealth.com - Inclusive Therapists: inclusivetherapists.com - BEAM: beam.community - Open Path Collective: openpathcollective.org - NAMI (National Alliance on Mental Illness): nami.org - Sista Afya: sistafya.org - The Loveland Foundation: thelovelandfoundation.org - Boris Lawrence Henson Foundation: borislhensonfoundation.org - Black Women's Health Imperative: bwhi.org - The Confess Project: theconfessproject.com - AAKOMA Project: aakomaproject.org - The Steve Fund: stevefund.org - NQTTCN: nqttcn.com - My Brother's Keeper Cares: mybrotherskeepercares.org - 988 Suicide & Crisis Lifeline: Call or text 988 - Black Mental Health Hotline: 1-866-244-7470 - Crisis Text Line: Text HOME to 741741 - SAMHSA National Helpline: 1-800-662-4357 - Trans Lifeline: (877) 565-8860 - The Trevor Project: 1-866-488-7386 - Find Community Health Centers: findahealthcenter.hrsa.gov - Check Medicaid Eligibility: healthcare.gov - SAMHSA Treatment Locator: findtreatment.gov - Black Mental

Wellness: blackmentalwellness.com - Ourselves Black: ourselvesblack.com - Therapy Helpers (Black Mental Health Resource Guide): therapyhelpers.com/blog/black-mental-health-resource-guide/ - Well Being Trust: wellbeingtrust.org

CHAPTER 6

Chapter 5 gave you the tools: how to find therapy, access care, protect yourself in crisis, build community, advocate for change. You have the resources.

Now comes the deeper work: creating a sustainable healing practice that fits YOUR life.

This isn't about following someone else's perfect wellness routine. Not about expensive spa days or Instagram-worthy self-care. This is about building real practices that actually work when life is hard.

When you're exhausted from working two jobs. When your family depends on you. When racism is relentless. When grief is overwhelming. When anxiety won't let you sleep. When depression makes everything feel pointless.

This chapter is about: - Understanding different therapy approaches and which might work for you - Creating daily practices you'll actually maintain - Reclaiming African American healing traditions - Integrating faith and mental health - Building a personalized wellness plan - Knowing when professional help is necessary You've learned the history. You've seen the system. You've found the resources. Now let's build your healing path.

When someone says "you should try therapy," what does that even mean?

There are dozens of therapy approaches. Understanding the differences helps you: - Ask therapists specific questions about their approach - Know what to expect in sessions - Choose therapies that match your needs - Understand why one therapist might use different methods than another Let's break down the main approaches, especially those most effective for trauma and mental health challenges common in Black communities.

What it is: Evidence-based treatment specifically designed for trauma survivors.

Combines cognitive behavioral techniques with trauma processing.

Particularly effective for complex trauma—the kind that comes from ongoing experiences like racism.

How it works: - Helps you identify and change thought patterns related to trauma - Gradually exposes you to trauma memories in safe, controlled way - Teaches coping skills for managing trauma responses - Includes family/support people when appropriate What happens in sessions: - Early sessions: Learn about trauma and its effects, develop coping skills - Middle sessions: Process traumatic memories through specific techniques - Later sessions: Practice new skills, prepare for future challenges Research shows: TF-CBT reduces PTSD symptoms with effect sizes of 1.37-2.81 (meaning very strong positive effects). A 2024 study found it worked across 12 sessions for both PTSD and complex PTSD.

Adaptations for Black Communities: TF-CBT has been adapted to include Racial Socialization (RS) components specifically for Black youth experiencing racism and trauma. This version (TF-CBT + RS) shows "significant positive impact" for Black young people.

Best for: - Trauma from specific incidents (violence, accidents, assault) - Ongoing racial trauma - Complex PTSD from cumulative experiences - When you want structured, goal-oriented approach Questions to ask therapists: "Have you been trained in TF-CBT?"

"Do you use the racial socialization adaptation for Black clients?"

"How many sessions does TF-CBT typically take?"

What it is: Trauma therapy that uses bilateral brain stimulation (typically eye movements) to help you reprocess traumatic memories. Sounds weird. It works.

How it works: - You recall traumatic event while tracking therapist's finger moving side to side (or using tones, taps) - The bilateral stimulation (left-right motion) "taxes working memory"

- This reduces vividness and emotional intensity of traumatic memories - Your brain reprocesses the memory with less distress What happens in sessions: - Phase 1-2: History-taking, preparation (learning coping skills) - Phase 3-4: Assessment, desensitization (actual eye movement work) - Phase 5-6-7: Installation of positive beliefs, body scan, closure - Phase 8: Re-evaluation in following sessions Research shows: Systematic review of 16 studies (2000-2023) confirmed EMDR significantly lowers PTSD symptoms. Effective for PTSD, anxiety, depression. Works faster than some talk therapies—often see results in 6-12 sessions.

Adaptations for trauma types: Ecotherapy-Informed EMDR combines traditional EMDR with cultural and ecological wisdom, described as "culturally responsive trauma treatment."

Particularly relevant for addressing environmental racism and community trauma.

Best for: - PTSD from specific traumatic events - Racial trauma incidents (police encounters, discrimination events) - When talking about trauma feels too overwhelming - When you've "talked about it" but still feel triggered Questions to ask therapists: "Are you certified in EMDR?"

"How do you adapt EMDR for racial trauma?"

"Do you offer remote EMDR?" (yes, this exists via apps/devices) What it is: Newly developed protocol specifically designed to treat racial stress and trauma in Black and other racialized communities. This was created FOR us, BY people who understand racism's impact.

How it works: Based on cognitive-behavioral approach but centered on anti-racism.

Includes: - Validating experiences of racism (not "is it really racism?") - Psychoeducation about racial trauma and its effects - Debunking myths about race and skin color (addressing "skin-tone trauma") - Narrative work (telling your story in supportive environment) - Cognitive restructuring (challenging internalized racism) - Emotion regulation skills - Building resilience and community connection What makes it different: - Explicitly asks about racial stressors (police encounters, workplace discrimination, hate crimes) - Recognizes that racism is TRAUMATIC (not just "stressful") - Therapist must be actively anti-racist - Acknowledges darker skin = more racism (skin-tone trauma) - Provides "true information" to counter racist narratives Research shows: Randomized controlled trial currently underway. Early results show "significant promise" for reducing racial trauma and depression symptoms, improving functioning.

Critical therapist requirements: - Anti-racist, empathy-centered approach - Familiar with common racial stressors - Won't dismiss or invalidate experiences - Won't assume disparities are "innate" or biological Best for: - Cumulative experiences of racism - When race is central to your mental health challenges - Skin-tone trauma - Medical racism trauma - Workplace discrimination - Police-related trauma Questions to ask therapists: "Are you trained in the Healing Racial Trauma Protocol?"

"How do you address racial trauma in your practice?"

"Do you have an explicitly anti-racist approach to therapy?"

What it is: Structured, goal-oriented approach focused on identifying and changing thought patterns that affect emotions and behaviors. Most researched therapy approach.

How it works: - Identify negative/unhelpful thought patterns - Challenge those thoughts with evidence - Replace with more balanced/realistic thoughts - Practice new behaviors based on new thoughts Example: - Thought: "I'm going to mess up this presentation and everyone will think I'm stupid"

- CBT process: Is this true? What's the evidence? What would I tell a friend thinking this?

- Alternative thought: "I've prepared well. Even if I'm nervous, I know this material. One presentation doesn't define me"

What happens in sessions: - Homework assignments (thought records, behavioral experiments) - Learning specific skills (challenging thoughts, problem-solving, relaxation) - Tracking progress on specific goals - Typically 12-20 sessions Best for: - Depression - Anxiety disorders - When you want structured, practical approach - When you like homework and tracking progress Limitations for Black clients: - Standard CBT doesn't address racism/discrimination - May pathologize normal responses to oppression - Works best when combined with cultural awareness Questions to ask therapists: "How do you adapt CBT for Black clients experiencing racism?"

"Do you address how discrimination affects thought patterns?"

What it is: Originally developed for borderline personality disorder but now used for anyone struggling with emotional regulation, self-harm, or intense mood swings.

How it works: Four skill modules: 1. Mindfulness: Being present without judgment 2. Distress Tolerance: Getting through crises without making things worse 3. Emotion Regulation: Understanding and managing intense emotions 4. Interpersonal Effectiveness: Maintaining relationships while respecting yourself What happens in sessions: - Weekly individual therapy - Weekly skills training group (learning the four modules) - Phone coaching between sessions (when in crisis) - Therapist consultation team (they get support too) Best for: - Emotional intensity that feels out of control - Self-harm or suicidal thoughts - Relationship problems - When you feel emotions MORE intensely than others seem to Why it helps Black people specifically: - Validates that intense emotions make sense given circumstances - Provides concrete skills for managing racism-triggered emotional responses - Interpersonal effectiveness helps navigate microaggressions - Distress tolerance for handling discrimination without self-destructive coping Questions to ask therapists: "Are you trained in DBT?"

"Do you offer both individual and group components?"

"How do you apply DBT to racial trauma?"

What it is: Instead of trying to eliminate painful thoughts/feelings, ACT teaches you to accept them while still living according to your values.

Core idea: "Pain is inevitable. Suffering is optional. The goal isn't to feel good—it's to live well."

Six core processes: 1. Acceptance: Making room for painful feelings 2. Cognitive Defusion: Noticing thoughts without believing them 3. Present Moment: Being here now 4. Self as Context: You are more than your thoughts 5. Values: What matters to you?

6. Committed Action: Do what matters even when it's hard Best for: - When positive thinking feels like toxic positivity - Chronic pain (physical or emotional) - When you're tired of "fighting" your feelings - Racism fatigue (accepting you can't control racism, choosing how you respond) Why it helps with racial trauma: - Acknowledges you can't "think positive" away racism - Focuses on what you CAN control (your responses, your values) - Validates pain while empowering action What it is: Therapy approach seeing personality as made up of different "parts" (like inner critic, wounded child, protector). Goal is internal harmony.

How it works: - Identify different parts (the perfectionist, the people-pleaser, the angry one) - Understand each part's positive intention (even harmful parts) - Heal wounded parts - Let "Self" (calm, compassionate core) lead Example for Black mental health: - Part that stays silent about racism: Protecting you from retaliation - Part that's always angry: Protecting your dignity - Part that overworks: Proving you're "good enough"

- Part that isolates: Protecting you from rejection Best for: - Understanding inner conflicts - Shame (especially internalized racism) - When different parts of you want different things - Complex trauma where you "split" to survive Growing popularity: 2025 data shows 2% of therapy seekers specifically searching for IFS— rising interest in understanding "inner critics, shame, or parts-based experiences of trauma."

What it is: Views problems as separate from people. You're not "a depressed person"— you're a person experiencing depression. Focuses on highlighting strengths and rewriting life narrative.

How it works: - Externalize the problem (depression is what you're dealing with, not who you are) - Identify unique outcomes (times you resisted the problem) - Re-author your story (what story do YOU want to tell about your life?) - Witness your story (sharing with others who validate it) Why it's powerful for Black people: - Separates YOU from racist narratives - Highlights resistance and resilience (ancestors survived—you're continuing that) - Challenges internalized oppression - Honors cultural stories and heritage Best for: - When you've internalized negative messages about Blackness - Feeling defined by trauma/diagnosis - Want to reclaim your story from those who tried to write it What it is: Therapy with 6-12 people facing similar challenges, led by trained therapist(s).

Types: - Process groups: Focus on here-and-now relationships in group - Psychoeducational groups: Learn specific skills (CBT skills, DBT skills) - Support groups: Share experiences, less therapist-led Why it works: - Realize you're not alone - Learn from others' experiences - Practice relationship skills in safe space - More affordable than individual therapy - Especially powerful for Black people (collective healing tradition) Best for: - Isolation, feeling like "only one"

- Learning from others facing similar challenges - Affordability - When you want community alongside professional guidance What it is: Approaches that work directly with body sensations, movement, and nervous system to heal trauma.

Types: - Somatic Experiencing: Focus on body sensations, release trapped trauma energy - Sensorimotor Psychotherapy: Process trauma through body awareness and movement - Body-oriented group therapy: Combine somatic techniques with group process Why body-based healing matters: - "Trauma is stored in the body"

- Talk therapy doesn't always reach body-level trauma - Racism creates physical stress responses (weathering) - African healing traditions include movement/dance What happens in sessions: - Notice body sensations (tightness, heat, tingling) - Track those sensations as they change - Use movement to release trauma - Learn to regulate nervous system Research shows: 2021 study found body-oriented group therapy effective for complex trauma. 2024 research confirms somatic techniques helpful for PTSD when combined with other approaches.

Best for: - When you "can't talk about it"

- Chronic body tension/pain linked to stress - Trauma stored in body (feeling it but can't articulate it) - When talk therapy hasn't been enough Taking care of yourself isn't a luxury. It's survival.

Think of mental health like your phone battery. Can't function running on 2%. Need to recharge regularly, not just when about to die.

These practices require: - No money - No special equipment - No appointments - Just you, right now Why it works: When anxious/stressed, breathing becomes shallow and fast. This tells brain you're in danger, creating MORE anxiety. Intentional breathing activates parasympathetic nervous system—your body's "calm down" button.

4-4-6-2 Breathing Technique: 1. Sit comfortably, feet flat, hands on thighs 2. One hand on chest, one on belly 3. Inhale through nose for 4 counts (belly expands, not chest) 4. Hold for 4 counts 5. Exhale through mouth for 6 counts (make "whoosh" sound) 6. Pause for 2 counts 7. Repeat 5 times When to use: - Before difficult conversations - During panic attacks - Can't sleep - After triggering events (news about police violence, microaggression) - Before you go off on someone who just disrespected you Do it now. Right now. Put the book down. One cycle. Feel your body remember how to be calm.

What exercise does for your brain: - Releases endorphins (natural mood boosters) - Increases serotonin and dopamine (happiness chemicals) - Reduces cortisol (stress hormone) - Improves sleep - Gives sense of accomplishment depression tries to steal - Gets you out of your head, into your body (where healing happens) The key: Find movement you ENJOY If you like being alone: - Walking (free, anywhere, anytime) - Jogging - Home workout videos (YouTube free) - Yoga - Swimming If you need community: - Group fitness classes - Sports teams (adult rec leagues) - Walking groups - Dance classes (Afrobeat, hip-hop, Zumba) - Church fitness groups If you have limited mobility: - Chair yoga - Water aerobics - Gentle stretching - Tai chi - Seated dance If you're on tight budget: - Walking (free) - Dancing in your living room (free) - YouTube workouts (free) - Bodyweight exercises (free) Start small: 10 minutes TODAY. Don't wait for perfect conditions.

Poor sleep makes EVERYTHING worse: Depression, anxiety, irritability, concentration, physical health, immune function, ability to cope with racism.

Sleep Hygiene (Actually Follow These): Timing: - Same bedtime and wake time EVERY DAY (yes, weekends too) - If you can't fall asleep in 20 minutes, get up and do something calm, then try again Environment: - Room temp: 65-68°F - Dark (blackout curtains or sleep mask) - Quiet (earplugs or white noise if needed) - Comfortable (good mattress/pillows if possible) Technology: - NO screens 1 hour before bed (blue light blocks melatonin) - Charge phone in another room (or at least across room) - No TV in bedroom Substances: - No caffeine after 2 PM (stays in system 6-8 hours) - Limit alcohol (disrupts sleep quality) - Avoid large meals right before bed Wind-Down Routine (30 minutes before bed): - Dim lights - Gentle stretching -

Reading (not on screen) - Prayer/meditation - Breathing exercises - Journal Use bed ONLY for sleep (and sex). Not work, TV, scrolling. Your brain needs to associate bed with rest.

If you try these for 2 weeks and still struggle, see a doctor. Sleep problems can signal depression, anxiety, sleep apnea, or other conditions needing treatment.

Your gut makes 90% of your body's serotonin. Gut health = mental health.

Foods That Help Mental Health: Omega-3 Fatty Acids (reduce depression): - Salmon, sardines, mackerel - Walnuts, flaxseed, chia seeds - If budget tight: canned fish, walnuts from dollar store Complex Carbohydrates (stabilize mood): - Whole grain bread, brown rice, quinoa - Sweet potatoes - Oats Protein (building blocks for brain chemicals): - Lean meats, fish - Beans, lentils (cheap!) - Eggs - Greek yogurt Leafy Greens (folate for mood): - Collard greens, kale, spinach - Turnip greens - (Our traditional foods!) Fermented Foods (gut health): - Yogurt - Kimchi, sauerkraut - Pickles Foods That Hurt Mental Health: - Too much sugar (crashes, mood swings) - Highly processed foods (lack nutrients brain needs) - Excessive alcohol (depresses nervous system, disrupts sleep) - Too much caffeine (triggers/worsens anxiety) Real talk about soul food: Mac and cheese, fried chicken, cornbread, sweet potato pie—these connect us to our roots, our people, our heritage. Don't give them up. Balance is key. Sunday dinner with family? Enjoy every bite. But Tuesday breakfast can be oats with walnuts. You can honor your culture AND take care of your body. Both things can be true.

Loneliness is as harmful to health as smoking 15 cigarettes a day.

Your body literally treats loneliness as physical threat.

When energy is LOW: - Text someone you've been thinking about them - Join online support groups (watch/read until ready to talk) - Call/FaceTime while doing something else (folding laundry, cooking) - Sit on porch/stoop where neighbors might pass by - Comment on social media posts from people you actually know When you have MORE energy: - Church services or faith community events - Book club, game night, hobby group - Volunteer (helping others helps us) - Take a class (in-person or online) - Host small gathering (nothing fancy—pizza and conversation) - Join sports league or fitness class - Community events (festivals, forums, town halls) - Start support group for others with similar challenges Quality over quantity: One real friendship helps mental health more than dozens of surface connections. One person who really SEES you is worth more than 100 followers.

Social media can connect us to support, resources, community. But it can also harm.

You know technology is hurting when: - Comparing yourself to others' highlight reels - Doom-scrolling negative news for hours - FOMO from seeing others' activities - "Just one more video" turns into 3 hours gone - Liking posts instead of actually talking to people - Checking phone first thing in morning, last thing at night - Feeling worse after using social media To use technology intentionally: - Schedule offline time (put phone in another room) - Clean up your feeds (unfollow accounts that make you feel bad) - Turn off non-essential notifications (you don't need to know instantly about every like/comment) - Video calls with distant friends = good. Scrolling instead of calling friend 10 minutes away = not good - When with people, BE with them (phones away, eyes up, present) - Use "Do Not Disturb" liberally - Delete apps that waste your time (you can always reinstall if needed) Before therapy offices, before prescription medications, before psychiatric diagnoses, our ancestors had sophisticated healing practices that kept them whole through unspeakable trauma.

These aren't replacements for modern mental health care. They work ALONGSIDE it.

In West African tradition, griots kept history alive and helped people process trauma through stories.

Why storytelling heals: - Gives shape and meaning to chaotic experiences - Creates distance from overwhelming emotions (watching your story vs drowning in it) - Connects you to others with similar experiences - Your story might be someone else's lifeline Ways to practice storytelling: Journaling: - 10 minutes daily - Stream-of-consciousness (no editing, no judging) - "Morning pages" (write 3 pages first thing in morning) - Gratitude journals - Trauma journals (but balance with positive too) Voice Memos: - Talk to your phone like talking to friend - Sometimes speaking easier than writing - Can listen back later (or not) Sharing with Trusted People: - Friends who "get it"

- Support groups - Therapist - Family members who are safe Creative Expression: - Poetry (doesn't have to rhyme or be "good") - Music (write songs, rap, sing) - Art (paint, draw, collage) - When words aren't enough, create From work songs that transformed oppression into rhythm, to gospel that turns pain into praise, to dancing it out—sound and movement have ALWAYS been African American medicine.

Why it works scientifically: - Music therapy reduces anxiety and depression - Dancing releases trauma stored in body - Drumming synchronizes brain waves, creates group connection - Singing releases endorphins, improves breathing Make healing playlists: - Sad songs when you need to cry: Let yourself feel it - Uplifting songs when you need hope: Gospel, soul, whatever lifts you - Anger songs when you're furious: Let it OUT (safely) - Calm songs for anxiety: Instrumental, nature sounds, lo-fi Sing: - In shower - In car - In church choir - Alone (nobody's judging) - Singing releases endorphins, helps breathing Dance alone: - Put on music and move however your body wants - This isn't about looking good—it's about releasing emotion trapped in muscles - Let your body tell its story - Shake, jump, sway, spin Go to live music: - Church services - Concerts - Open mic nights - Shared musical experiences create connection words can't touch Make music: - Drumming - Singing - Playing instruments - No skill required—it's about expression, not perfection Before pharmaceutical companies, there were healing plants.

Modern science now confirms what traditional healers knew.

Herbs That Can Help (WITH CAUTIONS): Chamomile: - Reduces anxiety - Improves sleep - Safest as tea - Generally very safe Lavender: - Calms nervous system -

Helps with stress - Use: tea, essential oil, dried herb in pillows Peppermint: - Eases stress-related stomach issues - Improves focus - Tea or essential oil Lemon Balm: - Reduces anxiety - Lifts mood - Tea form Ashwagandha: - Adaptogen (helps body handle stress) - Capsule or powder form - Don't take if pregnant/breastfeeding

CRITICAL CAUTIONS:

Natural ≠ Safe: - Herbs can interact with medications - Quality matters—buy from reputable sources (not gas stations) - Can have side effects - Some dangerous if pregnant/breastfeeding These ADD to necessary medications, DON'T replace them: - If you're on psychiatric medications, talk to doctor BEFORE adding herbs - Don't stop prescribed medications to "try herbs instead"

- Combination of medication + herbs might work better than either alone Where to learn more safely: - Certified herbalists - Integrative medicine doctors - Books by respected herbalists - National Center for Complementary and Integrative Health (nccih.nih.gov) In African cultures, mental health wasn't just individual problem. If someone struggled, community gathered around them.

"It takes a village" wasn't just about raising children. It was about

EVERYTHING.

Modern applications of collective care: Mutual Aid Networks: - Share resources with neighbors - Skill sharing (childcare, meals when someone's struggling) - Financial cooperation (crowdfunding, collective savings) - Nobody survives alone Church Mental Health Ministries: - Many African American churches creating mental health programs - Blend spiritual support with mental health awareness - Trained lay counselors - Peer support groups - Reducing stigma from pulpit Support Groups for Black Folks: - PTSD support - Depression support - Grief support - Parenting support - Whatever you're facing, you're not alone Regular Honest Conversations: - Friends where it's safe to say "I'm not okay"

- Get support, not judgment - Check-ins (not just "how are you?" but really asking) Gathering to Process Shared Trauma: - After police violence - After community loss - After collective experiences (elections, court verdicts, national events) - Process TOGETHER what affects us all The key: Creating spaces where vulnerability is safe, suffering isn't shameful, support is abundant.

For many African Americans, faith and church community are central to wellbeing. The Black church has been source of strength, connection, survival through: -

Slavery - Jim Crow - Civil Rights Movement - Ongoing oppression The church has: - Provided sanctuary when world was hostile - Offered hope when circumstances seemed hopeless - Created community when society segregated us - Preserved culture and heritage - Fostered leadership and activism This is real. This is powerful. This has kept us alive.

Some religious communities—not all, but some—have: - Made mental illness seem like lack of faith - Suggested prayer can replace needed medication - Shamed people for getting professional help - Used scripture to dismiss real psychological suffering - Told people depression was demon they needed to cast out - Created shame around mental health struggles This is harmful. This keeps people suffering. This can be deadly.

They can work together beautifully: You can: - Pray AND take medication - Trust God AND see therapist - Have strong faith AND struggle with depression - Believe in healing AND need professional treatment - Be spiritual AND have mental illness Faith doesn't mean you won't have mental health challenges. Biblical figures struggled: - Elijah's depression after mountaintop experience (1 Kings 19) - David's mood swings throughout Psalms - Job's trauma and suffering - Jesus's anguish in Garden of Gethsemane Taking care of the mind God gave you is STEWARDSHIP, not weakness.

Look for churches/religious communities that: - Have mental health ministries - Partner with mental health professionals - Discuss mental health from pulpit (not just in whispers) - Make space for real struggle (not just victory testimonies) - See therapy and medication as God's provision, not lack of faith - Support members getting professional help - Provide practical support (meals, childcare, financial help when someone's struggling) Questions to ask when looking for faith community: - "How does your church address mental health?"

- "Do you have mental health ministry or support groups?"

- "Can you recommend therapists who respect faith?"

If faith is part of your healing journey, you need therapist who: - Respects your spiritual beliefs (even if they don't share them) - Can blend faith into treatment if you want - Won't use religion to AVOID necessary clinical treatment - Won't dismiss your faith as "coping mechanism" needing to be challenged - Sees spiritual struggles as real (not just symptoms to eliminate) Questions to ask therapists about faith: - "How do you incorporate spirituality into treatment?"

- "Are you comfortable discussing my faith as part of therapy?"

- "How do you view the relationship between faith and mental health?"

Therapists who say: - "Faith has no place in therapy" = probably not good fit - "Just pray harder" = definitely not good fit - "I respect your faith and can include it if you'd like, while also providing clinical treatment" = might be good fit If Faith Is NOT Part of Your Journey: That's valid too. You don't have to be religious to heal. You don't have to forgive to move forward. You don't have to find "meaning" in your pain.

Secular healing is completely valid. There are many paths to wellness.

Mental wellness isn't universal. What works for someone else might not work for you.

Your wellness plan must fit: - Your life (schedule, responsibilities, resources) - Your values (what matters to YOU) - Your needs (your specific mental health challenges) - Your preferences (what you'll actually do consistently) Your wellness plan should include practices at different frequencies: Examples: - Take prescribed medication (same time daily) - 5-10 minute walk - 5 minute breathing practice - Drink water first thing in morning - Text one person - Journal for 5 minutes - Morning routine - Evening wind-down Keep it realistic. What will you ACTUALLY do every day? Start there.

Examples: - Therapy appointment (Tuesdays at 6 PM) - Support group (Thursdays) - Church service (Sundays) - Meal with friend or family member - Longer exercise session (30-60 minutes) - Therapy homework - Batch cooking healthy meals - Social activity Pick practices that create structure and connection.

Examples: - Review what's working and what isn't - Adjust your plan - Schedule next month's social activities - Replenish self-care supplies (herbs, journals, etc.) - Check in with yourself: "How am I REALLY doing?"

- Vision board or goal-setting - Financial check-in (money stress affects mental health) This is when you assess and adapt.

Examples: - Call therapist or crisis line - Use breathing techniques - Text your support person (name and number written down) - Go to crisis stabilization center (if available) - Use your crisis plan from Chapter 5 - Remove means (if having suicidal thoughts) - Go to ER if necessary (bring advocate if possible) Have this written down BEFORE crisis. Can't think clearly when in crisis.

Here's an example (yours will look different):

DAILY:

- Medication: 8 AM with breakfast - Morning: Wake 7 AM, drink water, breathe 5 minutes, walk 10 minutes - Evening: Wind down 9 PM (no screens, read, breathe), bed 10 PM - Throughout day: Notice when stressed, use breathing

WEEKLY:

- Tuesday 6 PM: Therapy - Thursday 7 PM: NAMI support group - Sunday 11 AM: Church - Friday evening: Meal with sister - Saturday: 30-minute workout

MONTHLY:

- First Sunday: Review plan, journal about what's working - Schedule social activities for next month - Buy groceries for healthy meals - Refill medications

EMERGENCY:

1. Call therapist: [phone number] 2. Text support person (Marcus): [phone number] 3. Crisis line: 988 or 1-866-244-7470 4. Breathing exercises 5. If having suicidal thoughts: Remove means, don't be alone, call crisis line immediately Step 1: Start Small Don't create elaborate plan

you'll abandon in 3 days. Pick ONE practice for each time scale.

Step 2: Write It Down - On your fridge - In your phone - Wherever you'll actually see it Step 3: Share with Support People So they know how to help you Step 4: Expect to Adjust Life changes. Your plan should too. That's not failure—that's adaptation.

Step 5: Be Specific Not "exercise more" → "Walk 10 minutes at 7:30 AM"

Not "eat better" → "Oatmeal with walnuts for breakfast Monday-Friday"

Step 6: Remove Barriers - Lay out workout clothes night before - Put vitamins next to coffee pot - Set phone reminders - Make it EASY to do the thing Step 7: Track What Works Notice what actually helps. Do more of that. Let go of what doesn't work.

Real talk: Some mental health conditions REQUIRE professional treatment.

You wouldn't try to treat diabetes with meditation alone. Wouldn't set broken bone with affirmations. Mental illness is medical illness.

Self-care and traditional practices are valuable. But they're not replacements for professional treatment when you have: - Major depression - Bipolar disorder - Schizophrenia - Severe anxiety disorders

- PTSD

- Suicidal thoughts - Psychosis - Eating disorders You need professional help if: - You're having thoughts of suicide or self-harm - You're hearing voices or seeing things others don't - Your mood swings are extreme (very high then very low) - You can't function in daily life (can't work, can't care for yourself, can't get out of bed) - You've lost interest in everything you used to enjoy - You're using substances to cope - Your anxiety is constant and overwhelming - You're having panic attacks - You've experienced significant trauma - Self-care practices aren't helping - Things are getting worse despite your efforts You might benefit from professional help if: - You feel stuck - You want to understand yourself better - You're navigating major life transitions - Your relationships are suffering - You're dealing with grief - You want to process past experiences - You're interested in personal growth Professional help doesn't mean you're weak. It means you're wise enough to get the right tools for the job.

Our ancestors survived the unsurvivable: - Middle Passage - Slavery - Jim Crow - Lynching - Redlining - Mass incarceration - Police violence They kept their humanity when the world tried to crush it. They passed down: - Healing traditions - Stories - Survival strategies - Culture - Music - Food - Faith - Resilience They didn't do all that just so we could survive. They did it so we could THRIVE.

Your healing is an act of resistance.

Every time you: - Take care of your mental health → You're fighting systems that tried to break you - Seek help → You're breaking silence that kept community sick - Practice self-care → You're claiming your right to peace - Choose therapy → You're refusing to let trauma define you - Build community → You're creating what systems tried to destroy The system wants you broken, isolated, hopeless. Your healing is revolutionary.

Your healing is an act of love.

For yourself: - You deserve peace - You deserve joy - You deserve rest - These aren't things you have to earn—they're your BIRTHRIGHT For your family: - Break cycles of trauma - Model healthy coping - Be present for those you love - Show them healing is possible For your community: - When you heal, you show others it's possible - Your healing creates ripples - Healed people help heal others For generations after you: - Interrupt intergenerational trauma - Pass down resilience AND healing - Give them what you didn't have Healing isn't a straight line: - Some days: two steps forward - Some days: one step back - Some days: feel like going backwards entirely That's normal. That's expected. That's part of the process.

Healing is: - Messy - Hard - Non-linear - Worth it

- POSSIBLE

You deserve: - Peace - Joy - To feel good in your body and mind - Support when struggling - Celebration when thriving - Rest, softness, gentleness These aren't things you earn. They're your birthright as human being.

You don't need: - Perfect plan - Lots of money - Ideal circumstances - More time You need: - To start - One practice - One step - Right now Your healing journey begins with single step. That step can be as simple as: - Taking deep breath right now - Deciding you deserve better - Reading this chapter - Saving crisis number in phone - Texting one person Start where you are. Use what you have. Do what you can.

Because you deserve healing. You deserve peace. You deserve joy.

The well is running. But it doesn't have to run dry. Not for you. Not anymore.

CHAPTER 7

You've learned your history. Chapter 2 showed you where this crisis came from—slavery's trauma, medical experimentation, generations of broken promises.

You've seen the current reality. Chapter 3 laid out the numbers, the barriers, the systematic exclusion from care.

You understand the deadly system. Chapter 4 showed you how police response kills people who need help, how the system is designed for control, not care.

You know how to access help. Chapter 5 gave you resources, directories, crisis plans, concrete action steps.

You're building your healing practice. Chapter 6 taught you therapy modalities, daily practices, how to create sustainable wellness.

Now comes the hardest truth: Personal healing isn't enough.

You can go to therapy. Take your medication. Practice self-care. Build your support network. And that's essential. But while you're healing yourself, the system is still killing people.

Deborah Danner is still dead. Walter Wallace Jr. is still dead. Kayla Moore is still dead. And more people are dying right now. Today. While you read this.

Andrea Clark is still dead. Porter Burks is still dead. The names keep coming. The body count keeps rising.

Personal healing AND systemic change. Not either/or. Both.

This chapter is about what happens when individuals become community, when community becomes movement, when movement forces change.

This is about the power we have together that we don't have alone.

Nearly 1 in 10 U.S. adults experienced a mental health crisis in the past year. That's according to nationally representative data collected in spring 2025. Not a crisis like "bad day"—a crisis where thoughts, feelings, or behaviors were too much to handle and required prompt assistance.

Black Americans are hit harder: - 11.8% of Black adults reported mental health crisis in past year - Compared to 7.4% of white adults - 21.4% of Black adults experience mental illness annually - 19.7% experienced mental health condition in past year (2024 data) Young Black adults suffering most: - 15.1% of adults 18-29 experienced crisis -

Compared to 2.6% of those over 60 Depression and anxiety epidemic: - 10.3% of Black adults experienced moderate to severe depression (vs 8.9% national average) - 18.6% experienced anxiety (vs 12.5% national average) Housing instability catastrophic: - 37.9% of people experiencing housing instability reported mental health crisis - Homelessness and mental illness creating deadly cycle Of those who experienced crisis, 72.6% sought help. That sounds good until you see WHERE they sought help: Fewer than 1 in 5 used formal crisis services: - 988 hotline - Mobile crisis teams - Crisis stabilization centers Most turned to: - Outpatient providers (if they could get appointments) - Emergency rooms (8-hour waits for 5-minute evaluations) - Informal supports (friends, family, church) - 911/Police (often with deadly results) For Black Americans specifically: Persistent underutilization of crisis hotlines. Even as national call volume increased 283%, Black callers consistently underrepresented.

Why the gap? "Black, Hispanic, and low-income communities often prefer informal, peer-based, or community-oriented supports over formal crisis services."

Translation: We don't trust the system. And we have good reasons not to.

Research from 2010-2025 reveals disturbing pattern: Calls involving Black individuals disproportionately escalated to 911 for "active rescue."

- 53% of calls involving Black individuals led to police involvement - Far exceeding our 32% of population - "Active rescue" = police sent, often armed response This means: Black people in crisis are more likely to have police show up when they call for help. More likely to be seen as "dangerous" requiring police. More likely to end up in handcuffs or body bags instead of getting treatment.

The system designed to help us often harms us instead.

Mobile Crisis Teams (MCTs) are expanding nationwide: 2024 Statistics: - Operating in 100% of responding states (all 50 states) - 206% increase in clients served (2022-2024) - 56% increase in number of programs - 195% increase in state expenditures Scale achieved: - 25 states able to report served over 203,000 people in one state (Illinois) to as few as 196 (New Mexico) - 24% were under age 18, 76% adults - Most teams respond to both mental health and substance use crises Federal investment growing: - $1.3 billion awarded (2021-2024) specifically for crisis response - Additional $2.3 billion for general behavioral health (including crisis) - $45 million for Community Crisis

Response Partnership (2022-2024) - 988 Lifeline received nearly 16 million contacts since 2022 launch On average across reporting states: - 64.3% of dispatches successfully resolved during contact (no additional intensive follow-up needed) - 33.3% referred to outpatient care - 12.9% needed crisis stabilization center - 15% required hospital Compare to police response: - Arrests - Jail - Force - Death CAHOOTS (Eugene, Oregon)—30+ Years of Proof: - Responds to 20% of 911 calls - Over 200,000 crisis calls handled since inception - Zero fatalities - Less than 1% require police backup - Cost savings pay for program multiple times over STAR (Denver, Colorado)—Born from Black Lives Matter: - Launched June 2020 in response to protest demands - Zero arrests in first year - Zero police backup needed - 33% reduction in crime in service area (yes, crime DROPPED when they sent therapists) - $20,000 saved per call This isn't theory. This is proven. This works.

Despite expansion, massive gaps persist: Only 40% of U.S. counties have at least one MCT (2024 study) - 60% of counties have ZERO mobile crisis services - Rural areas especially underserved - Black communities in those areas have no alternatives to police Over 50% of MCTs lack scale to provide 24/7 availability - Mental health crises don't respect business hours - Monday-Friday 9-5 is not enough - Nights, weekends, holidays = back to police response Only 20.8% of mental health facilities offer mobile crisis services (2025 study of 9,036 facilities) - Most facilities still don't provide crisis response - Limited availability, geographic reach - Persistent staffing challenges State adoption of Medicaid enhancement slow: - By September 2024, only 21 states opted into enhanced federal matching for mobile crisis under ARPA - Despite federal government offering to pay MORE for these services - Politics and bureaucracy blocking expansion Law enforcement remains primary collaboration partner across MCT programs nationwide.

Why this is complicated: - Some argue law enforcement provides safety/security during response - But many communities—especially Black communities—feel UNSAFE when police present - History of trauma during police interactions - Police presence can escalate, not de-escalate Research finding: "Minoritized and historically oppressed communities and others who have frequently experienced trauma during police interactions have described feeling unsafe when law enforcement are present as part of mental health response."

The solution: Localities need range of MCT options: - Civilian-only teams (NO police) - Co-responder models (police + clinician) ONLY when necessary - Clearly defined triage criteria (transparent to public) - Police involvement limited to extreme cases: active violence, loaded firearms

Current reality: Too many programs still default to police involvement, especially for Black communities.

Every \$1 invested in mental health treatment returns \$4 in reduced healthcare costs and increased productivity.

Mobile crisis response costs LESS than police response: - Police response → expensive ER visits → incarceration - Mobile crisis → treatment connection → stability Crisis stabilization centers cost LESS than: - Emergency rooms - Psychiatric hospitals - Jails Early intervention returns $10 for every $1 spent: - Prevents more serious, expensive problems later - School-based mental health services - Community health centers - Prevention programs Supported housing costs LESS than: - Cycling people through shelters - Repeated jail stays - Emergency services - Hospitals Employment support programs: - Increase tax revenue - Reduce public assistance costs - Create economic productivity LA County Jail = largest mental health facility in United States.

Not by design. By default.

Any given day: - 17,000 people incarcerated - 5,000 have serious mental illness Cost to incarcerate one person with mental illness: $42,000/year - 5,000 people = $210 million/year - Doesn't include police costs, court costs, ER visits, lost productivity - Total actual cost: Over $400 million annually 2020 RAND Corporation study examined alternative: Scenario: $100 million annual investment in: - Mobile crisis teams countywide - Crisis stabilization centers - Supported housing for 1,000 people with serious mental illness - Intensive case management - Peer support services Projected results over 5 years: - 3,200 fewer people with mental illness incarcerated - 15,000 fewer arrests - 8,000 fewer ER visits - 2,100 fewer hospitalizations - Significant reduction in homelessness Financial impact: - Cost of investment: $100 million/year = $500 million over 5 years - Savings: $165 million/year = $825 million over 5 years - NET SAVINGS: $325 million over 5 years Not counting increased tax revenue from employment, prevented deaths, improved quality of life.

Read the report. Officials praised it. Board of Supervisors expressed support.

Then allocated $25 million—one-quarter of recommended investment.

Split across multiple pilot programs too small to achieve scale. Attached bureaucratic requirements delaying implementation. Failed to coordinate across departments.

Result: - LA County Jail STILL America's largest psychiatric facility - Thousands still cycling through jails rather than getting treatment - Taxpayers still spending hundreds of millions on incarceration that makes mental illness worse The Lesson: Economic case for mental health investment is overwhelming.

Politics and bureaucracy block implementation. It's not about affordability. It's about priorities.

African American community faced severe disparities: - 3x more likely to be arrested during mental health crises than white residents - 2x more likely to be hospitalized involuntarily - 50% less likely to receive outpatient mental health care - Significant distrust of mental health systems (for good reason) Medicaid expansion with enhanced mental health coverage: - Eliminated waiting lists for mental health services - Increased reimbursement rates (so providers could afford Medicaid patients) - Added coverage for peer support services - Covered culturally specific treatments Investment in African American mental health organizations: - $5 million specifically allocated to Black community-based providers - Multi-year funding commitments (not one-time grants) - Flexibility to design programs based on community needs - Let Black people lead Black healing Mobile crisis expansion: - Expanded CAHOOTS statewide - Created culturally specific crisis teams in Portland serving Black communities - Implemented 988 with immediate access to services (not just referrals) Criminal justice diversion: - Mental health courts in every major county - Jail diversion programs (treatment instead of booking) - Expungements of mental health-related charges upon program completion Crisis response: - 40% reduction in police shootings of individuals with mental health crises statewide - In Portland's Black community: 60% reduction - 60% fewer Black people killed Incarceration: - 35% reduction in jail bookings for mental health-related charges in Black communities - Treatment, not cages Access to care: - 200% increase in Black folks receiving outpatient mental health services - Average wait time: 6 weeks → 3 days Outcomes: - 45% decrease in hospital readmission rates for mental health crises - 28% increase in employment among people receiving services - People getting better, working, living Cost: - Despite significant investment, Oregon saved money overall - Reduced ER use, reduced incarceration, increased productivity - Doing the right thing saved money Before reforms: - Age 28, PTSD and depression from police violence - Arrested 3 times for disorderly conduct during crises - Each arrest made conditions worse - No insurance, no consistent care - Cycling: crisis → jail → release → crisis → jail After reforms: - Qualified for Medicaid, got provider within a week - During next crisis: Culturally specific mobile team responded (including Black peer specialist) - NO police - Connected to trauma-focused therapy designed for police violence survivors - Joined peer support group for Black men - After 6 months: Found employment, crisis-free 18 months

Marcus's transformation happened because Oregon created systems supporting recovery rather than criminalizing illness.

Oregon's success proves investment works when it's: - Adequately funded (not just pilot programs) - Sustained over time (not cut when budgets tighten) - Culturally specific (not one-size-fits-all) - Community-led (not imposed from outside) - Comprehensive (addressing multiple barriers simultaneously) If Oregon can do this, EVERY state can.

The question isn't whether it's possible. It's whether governments care enough about Black lives to make it happen.

After several high-profile police killings of residents experiencing mental health crises, Detroit announced plans for mobile crisis response program.

Community advocates celebrated.

Media praised the city's "progressive approach."

Then nothing happened for four years.

2017: City officials still planning 2018: Budget included NO funding 2019: Pilot program announced but never launched 2020: COVID-19 pandemic delayed plans further During those four years of planning and delays: - At least 12 Detroiters experiencing mental health crises killed by police - Thousands more arrested rather than connected to treatment - Emergency rooms overwhelmed - Communities suffering without resources Not technical. Political and bureaucratic: - Police union opposition (feared losing funding) - Lack of political will (other things mattered more) - Bureaucratic inertia (departments couldn't coordinate) - No sustained community pressure (initial momentum faded, people stopped paying attention) Finally in 2021: After George Floyd's murder sparked renewed focus on alternatives to police, Detroit launched pilot program.

Five years after initially announcing it.

Five years of dead bodies while they planned.

Porter was 20 years old. Black. Experiencing mental health crisis.

Holding a knife.

Family called for help. Detroit's pilot program wasn't available that day— limited hours, limited coverage.

Police responded. Five officers shot Porter.

He was hit 38 times.

If Detroit had implemented mobile crisis response when first announced in 2016, Porter might be alive.

The Human Cost of Delay: Every year government waits is another year of preventable deaths. Detroit's delay killed people. Your city's delay is killing people right now.

1. Mental Health Crisis Response Act - Require all jurisdictions to implement mobile crisis teams (not suggest) - Provide federal funding for startup and operations - Set national standards for team composition, training, response - Mandate data collection and public reporting - Penalize jurisdictions with high rates of police violence during crises 2. National Mental Health Parity Enforcement - Create dedicated enforcement agency with REAL power - Conduct surprise audits of insurance companies - Impose significant fines for violations (penalties that actually hurt) - Allow individuals to sue for parity violations - Public reporting of compliance rates (name and shame) 3. Mandatory Medicaid Expansion - Federal requirement ALL states expand (no opt-outs) - Increased federal funding for expansion populations - Higher reimbursement rates for mental health services - Eliminate bureaucratic barriers to enrollment 4. Decriminalization of Mental Illness - Federal incentives for diversion programs - Prohibition on solitary confinement for people with mental illness - Mandatory mental health screening/treatment in jails and prisons - Expungement of mental health-related criminal records 5. Research Funding That Actually Helps Us - Increased NIH funding for mental health research - Requirements for representative research

samples (stop studying only white college students) - Dedicated funding for research on mental health in Black communities - Research on racism-related trauma and effective treatments 1. Mobile Crisis Teams Everywhere - 24/7 response capability - Coverage throughout jurisdiction (not just pilot programs) - Teams reflect communities they serve (cultural/linguistic diversity) - Integration with 911 dispatch - Adequate funding for staffing, equipment, operations 2. Crisis Stabilization Centers in Every Community - Short-term facilities (24-72 hours) - Immediate access (no waiting) - Professional staffing + peer support - Integration with ongoing services - Transportation provided 3. Fund Community Mental Health Centers Properly - Eliminate waitlists - Same-day or next-day appointments for urgent situations - Comprehensive services (therapy, meds, case management, peer support) - Competitive salaries to retain staff - Accept ALL insurance including Medicaid 4. Mental Health Services in Every School - Mental health professionals in EVERY school (not just rich ones) - Universal screening - Early intervention programs - Trauma-informed practices - Connection to community services 5. Housing First Programs - Stable housing without requiring sobriety/treatment first - Supportive housing with services - Rapid rehousing to prevent homelessness - Rental assistance - Anti-discrimination enforcement 6. Employment Support That Works - Job training and placement - Supported employment with job coaches - Anti-discrimination enforcement - Reasonable accommodations (flexible schedules, mental health days) - Financial support during treatment Reading isn't enough. Understanding isn't enough. Even agreeing change is needed isn't enough.

Change requires collective action. Organized power. Sustained pressure.

1. Get Informed - Learn about mental health issues in Black communities - Understand how policies affect access and outcomes - Know your elected officials and where they stand - Follow organizations doing advocacy work - Listen to people with lived experience 2. Take Care of Your Own Mental Health FIRST - You can't pour from empty cup - You can't fight for others if you're falling apart - Seek help if struggling - Practice self-care - Model help-seeking for others 3. Support Others in Your Circle - Check in on people you care about - Listen without judgment - Offer practical help (rides, childcare, meals) - Connect people to resources - Speak openly about mental health 4. Organize in Your Community - Join or start advocacy groups - Partner with existing organizations (NAMI, MHA, community groups) - Host community conversations - Create peer support groups - Pressure local officials - Don't just talk about it. Be about it.

5. Demand Accountability From Elected Officials - Contact representatives about mental health - Attend city council and county board meetings - Vote based on mental health positions - Organize campaigns around specific policies - Hold officials accountable for promises - Make mental health a voting issue - Make them care because their jobs depend on it 6. Support Black-Led Organizations - Donate money to organizations doing mental health work - Volunteer time and skills - Share their work on social media - Connect people to their resources - Let them lead (don't try to take over) - Trust Black people to know what Black people need 7. Use Your Platform - Share mental health information on social media - Tell your story if comfortable (reduces stigma) - Challenge stigmatizing language - Amplify voices of people with lived experience - Educate others about disparities - Advocate publicly for policy changes - Use whatever platform you have—big or small—to make noise Healthcare Providers: - Get trained in cultural competence and trauma-informed care - Accept Medicaid patients - Offer sliding-scale fees - Locate practice in underserved communities - Hire diverse staff - Partner with community organizations Researchers: - Include Black communities in research - Study what actually affects us - Make findings accessible - Partner with Black researchers - Return findings to communities - Support policy changes based on evidence Educators: - Teach about mental health in schools - Provide

resources to students/families - Recognize trauma in classroom - Connect students to services - Advocate for school-based mental health - Create safe spaces for difficult conversations Faith Leaders: - Discuss mental health from pulpit - Partner with mental health professionals - Create mental health ministries - Train lay leaders to recognize crisis - Reduce stigma in faith communities - Support members getting professional help Beyond policy, we need practical approaches that work with real people, real barriers, real lives.

1. Walk-In Crisis Services - No appointments needed (access help when you need it) - Located in communities (not intimidating medical campuses) - Staffed by people who reflect community - Integration with longer-term services 2. Community Health Workers - Trusted community members connecting people to resources - Cultural brokers navigating systems - Follow-up support professionals don't have time for - Bridge between formal healthcare and community 3. Faith-Based Partnerships - Recognition that many Black folks turn to faith communities first - Training for clergy and lay leaders - Partnerships between churches and mental health providers - Integration of spirituality into treatment when desired 4. Barbershops and Beauty Salons - Training for barbers/beauticians to recognize mental health concerns - Safe spaces for conversations - Connections to resources - Reducing stigma through trusted community spaces 5.

Cultural Programming - Arts programs promoting healing and expression - Cultural celebrations building community connection - Storytelling and oral history projects honoring experiences - Recreation and wellness addressing mind and body 6. Integration into Primary Care - Most people see primary care more than mental health specialists - Routine screening for depression, anxiety, trauma - Co-location of mental health providers in primary care - Warm hand-offs (introductions to mental health colleagues) - Treating mental health as part of overall health 7. Technology Done Right - Address digital divide FIRST - Teletherapy covered by insurance/Medicaid - Mental health apps designed WITH Black users - Online support groups and peer communities - Text-based crisis support - But always with human connection available - Technology complements, doesn't replace, human care 8. Peer Support - People with lived experience supporting others - Peer specialists employed in programs - Peer-run support groups - Recovery coaches navigating systems - Mentoring programs - Peer respite centers (alternatives to hospitalization) Why peer support works: - Peers understand challenges in ways professionals don't - Provide hope by modeling recovery - Reduce power imbalances - More trusted than professional providers - Increase engagement and improve outcomes 9. Trauma-Informed Care EVERYWHERE - Recognize trauma prevalence and impact - Screen for trauma histories - Avoid

re-traumatization through insensitive practices - Empower
people rather than control them - Build on strengths and
resilience - Create physically and emotionally safe
environments - Foster trust through transparency
Remember Andrea Clark from earlier in this chapter? 35
years old. Bipolar disorder. Died in Georgia jail because state
refused Medicaid expansion, didn't fund mobile crisis teams,
failed to provide adequate jail mental health care.

Andrea's death was preventable. Every policy failure
that killed her was a choice.

What happened after Andrea died?

Her family and community advocates formed
coalition demanding change: Actions taken: - Packed city
council meetings month after month - Organized rallies at
state capitol - Testified at legislative hearings - Created social
media campaign (#JusticeForAndrea) - Connected with
NAMI and Mental Health America - Built partnerships with
faith leaders - Mobilized voters around mental health issues -
Primary-challenged legislators who blocked reform Results
after 2 years of sustained pressure: - Georgia expanded
mobile crisis teams to Andrea's county - Improved jail
mental health screening and medication access - Banned
solitary confinement for people with mental illness in county
jail - Created crisis stabilization center - Hundreds of people

getting help who wouldn't have before Andrea is still dead. But fewer people will die the way she did.

That's the power of organized community action.

Remember Porter Burks? 20 years old. Shot 38 times by Detroit police during mental health crisis.

Porter's death galvanized community: Actions taken: - #JusticeForPorter movement - Weekly protests at police headquarters - Occupied city council chambers - Organized voter registration drives - Created coalition of families who lost loved ones to police violence during mental health crises - Demanded meeting with mayor - Worked with Detroit Disability Power to draft policy proposals - Made mobile crisis expansion THE issue in next election cycle Results after 18 months: - Detroit expanded pilot mobile crisis to 24/7 coverage citywide - Increased funding 400% - Created oversight board with community representatives - Required quarterly public reporting of outcomes - Police chief resigned, replaced with leader committed to crisis alternatives Porter is still dead. But Detroit's Black community forced change.

That's what sustained, organized pressure can do.

Across the country, similar stories: Louisville (after Jonathan Mattingly): Community organizing led to mobile crisis expansion, crisis stabilization center, civilian crisis response team.

Phoenix (after multiple police killings): Sustained pressure created cityfunded crisis response, reduced police mental health calls 35%.

Baltimore (after repeated tragedies): Organizing forced investment in community-based services, peer support programs, trauma-informed care system.

Every victory came from community organizing. Every change required sustained pressure. None of it happened because politicians decided to be nice.

They happened because communities made the status quo untenable.

When you advocate for change, you'll hear: "We can't afford it."

Response: We can't afford NOT to. Current system costs MORE.

Investment saves money. Plus, this isn't about affordability—it's about priorities. We find money for police militarization, tax cuts for wealthy, corporate subsidies. We can find money for mental health.

"Police just need better training."

Response: Police are not therapists. Can't turn warriors into healers with weekend workshop. We need different responders, not better-trained police.

Send mental health professionals to medical emergencies.

"These programs are experimental."

Response: CAHOOTS has 30+ years of proof. STAR shows clear results.

Oregon transformed their system. This isn't experimental—it's proven.

What's experimental is continuing to send police to mental health crises and expecting different results.

"What about public safety?"

Response: Mental illness isn't criminal activity. People in crisis need help, not handcuffs. Mobile crisis teams IMPROVE public safety—Denver saw 33% crime reduction. Safety means everyone survives the crisis, including the person needing help.

"We're already doing something."

Response: Pilot programs in limited areas aren't enough. 9-5 MondayFriday isn't enough. We need 24/7 coverage throughout jurisdiction. We need adequate funding. We need commitment, not gestures.

"This is political."

Response: Everything is political. People dying is political. Medicaid expansion is political. Funding priorities are political. The question is: which side are you on? The side that saves lives or the side that protects the status quo while bodies pile up?

They're not actually worried about affordability or feasibility.

They're worried about: - Loss of police funding/power - Admitting current approach is wrong (and deadly) - Accountability for past failures - Sharing power with community - Black people having voice in decisions - Change disrupting comfortable systems Your job: Make them more afraid of NOT changing than of changing.

Make inaction more costly than action. Make maintaining deadly systems politically untenable.

You've reached the end of this journey through the crisis.

Seven chapters. Seven stages of truth.

Chapter 1 showed you the human faces: Deborah, Walter, Kayla. Real people. Real deaths. You can't pretend you don't know their names now.

Chapter 2 taught you the history: Medical experimentation, slavery's trauma, generations of broken promises. This didn't start yesterday.

Chapter 3 gave you the numbers: The statistical crisis, the barriers, the systematic exclusion. You can't claim ignorance of the scope now.

Chapter 4 revealed the deadly system: Police response failures, training gaps, government inaction. You understand why calling 911 can be a death sentence.

Chapter 5 provided the resources: How to find therapy, access care, protect yourself in crisis. You have the tools to take action for yourself and help others.

Chapter 6 offered the healing paths: Therapy modalities, daily practices, cultural traditions, personalized wellness. You know how to build sustainable healing.

Chapter 7 showed you the power: What community organizing achieves, what's working, what's failing, what must change. You've seen proof that transformation is possible.

Now comes Chapter 8. The final chapter.

The question that determines whether any of this matters: What are YOU going to do about it?

Not what should someone do. Not what you hope happens. Not what you agree with in theory.

What are YOU going to do?

Because here's the final truth: You can't unknow what you know now.

You can't pretend Deborah, Walter, Kayla, Andrea, Porter don't exist. You can't claim you didn't know the history. You can't say no one told you about the barriers. You can't act surprised when the next person dies during a mental health crisis.

You know now.

And knowing creates responsibility.

The well is running dry. Chapter by chapter, you've traced it from its poisoned source through every barrier blocking its flow. You've seen the system designed to fail us. You've learned the tools for survival. You've witnessed the power of collective action.

The final chapter asks: Now that you know, what will you do?

Personal healing matters. Systemic change matters. Community power matters. All of it matters.

But only if you act.

Chapter 8 is your call to action. Your choice. Your commitment.

Everything that came before was preparation. Chapter 8 is what you do with what you've learned.

Turn the page when you're ready to answer that question.

When you're ready to stop being audience and become participant.

When you're ready to ensure the well doesn't run dry—not for you, not for your community, not for the generations coming after you.

The movement needs you. The work is waiting. The choice is yours.

What are YOU going to do about it?

CHAPTER 8

Seven chapters. Seven truths you can't unknow.

You met Deborah Danner, shot in her own home while holding scissors. You met Walter Wallace Jr., killed in front of his mother who begged police not to shoot. You met Kayla Moore, shot nine times while restrained in a hospital bed. You know their names now. You know their stories.

You learned the history—medical experimentation on Black bodies, slavery's intergenerational trauma, generations of broken promises from institutions designed to help us.

You saw the numbers—the statistical crisis, the barriers, the systematic exclusion, the deadly disparities that kill us at higher rates than everyone else.

You understand the system—how police response turns mental health crises into death sentences, how training gaps and government inaction maintain the status quo, how the system is designed for control instead of care.

You found the resources—specific directories, crisis numbers, concrete action steps to protect yourself and help others access care.

You learned the healing paths—therapy modalities, daily practices, cultural traditions, how to build sustainable wellness even in a system designed to break you.

You witnessed the power—Oregon's transformation, Detroit's movement, Andrea Clark Coalition's victory, proof that organized community action forces change when nothing else will.

Now comes the moment of truth.

Everything you've read up to this point was preparation. This chapter is what you do with what you've learned.

The question isn't "What should someone do?"

The question is: "What will YOU do?"

Not tomorrow. Not when you have more time. Not when circumstances are perfect.

What will you do today? Right now. Starting the moment you finish reading this sentence.

Because here's what I need you to understand: The well is still running dry.

Right now, while you're reading this, someone is in crisis. Someone is calling for help. Someone is calculating whether seeking assistance will get them killed. Someone is choosing between suffering in silence and risking police violence. Someone is dying.

You can't stop that by finishing this book and putting it on a shelf.

But you can stop SOME of it. If you act. If you commit. If you refuse to go back to pretending you don't know what you know now.

This chapter is about making that commitment real. About turning knowledge into action, understanding into movement, awareness into change.

This is where you decide who you're going to be in this fight.

Are you going to be someone who read a book and felt bad?

Or are you going to be someone who read a book and did something about it?

I know what you're thinking: "I'm just one person. What can I possibly do against systems this big, this broken, this entrenched?"

"I don't have time. I'm working two jobs. I'm taking care of family. I'm barely keeping my own head above water."

"I don't know how to organize. I'm not an activist. I've never done anything like this before."

"I'm dealing with my own mental health struggles. How can I help anyone else when I'm barely holding it together?"

I hear you. And I'm telling you: Start anyway.

You don't need: - To quit your job and become a full-time activist - A degree in public policy or social work - To be healed before you can help - To have all the answers - To be perfect - To do everything You need: - To do ONE thing - To start where you are - To use what you have - To begin today Pick ONE action from this list. Just one. Do it in the next 24 hours: 1. Save three numbers in your phone RIGHT NOW: - 988 (Suicide & Crisis Lifeline) - 1-866-244-7470 (Black Mental Health Hotline) - Text HOME to 741741 (Crisis Text Line) Do it now. Before you read another word. I'll wait.

Done? That's action. You just took the first step.

2. Text one person you care about: "Hey, I've been thinking about you. How are you really doing? Not 'I'm fine'—really."

Check on someone. Be the person who asks and actually listens. Do it today.

3. Share one resource on social media: Post about Therapy for Black Girls, Therapy for Black Men, NAMI support groups, 988 lifeline. One post. One share. Someone in your network needs it.

4. Register to vote (if you're not already): Mental health funding is decided by elected officials. Your vote is power.

Use it.

Go to vote.gov right now. Takes 5 minutes. Do it today.

5. Send one email to one elected official: Subject: "Mental Health Crisis Response Must Change"

Body: "I'm your constituent. I'm demanding you support mobile crisis teams staffed by mental health professionals, not police. People are dying. What are you doing about it?"

Copy, paste, send. Takes 2 minutes. Do it now.

6. Donate $5 to one organization: BEAM (Black Emotional & Mental Health Collective), Boris Lawrence Henson Foundation, The Loveland Foundation, NAMI.

Can't afford $5? That's okay. Share their work instead. Do one or the other today.

7. Have one conversation: Talk to one person about mental health. Your own experience, someone you're worried about, this book, why this matters. One real conversation.

This week.

Pick ONE. Not seven. ONE.

Do it in the next 24 hours.

That's how movements start. One person. One action. One day at a time.

You did one thing. Now let's build momentum.

Here's a 30-day plan that fits into your life. Not someone else's life.

YOUR life.

Day 1-2: Take care of YOU first - You read Chapter 6. Pick ONE daily practice and commit to it for 30 days.

- Breathing exercises, 10-minute walk, sleep hygiene— something.

- Write it down. Set phone reminder. Do it every day.

Day 3-4: Build your crisis plan - Chapter 5 gave you the template. Fill it out.

- Warning signs, coping strategies, people to call, what NOT to do.

- Share with one trusted person. Have it ready before you need it.

Day 5-7: Check on your people - Reach out to three people this week.

- Not "hey" texts. Real check-ins.

- "How are you really doing? What do you need?"

- Listen. Offer help. Connect to resources if needed.

Day 8-9: Find your group - Search for NAMI support group in your area - Look for Black mental health organizations - Check if your church has mental health ministry - Join one online support group - Show up. Even if just to listen at first.

Day 10-12: Learn your local landscape - Does your city have mobile crisis teams?

- Crisis stabilization centers?

- What happens when someone calls 911 during mental health crisis?

- Google: "[Your city] mental health crisis response"

- Know what exists. Know what's missing.

Day 13-14: Identify your officials - Who's your city council member? Mayor? County board?

- State representative? State senator?

- Find their contact info. Save it.

- Know who makes decisions that affect mental health in your community.

Day 15-17: Speak up online - Share one mental health resource per day on social media - Tell your own story if you're comfortable (reduces stigma) - Challenge one piece of stigmatizing language you see - Your voice matters. Use it.

Day 18-20: Speak up offline - Have three conversations about mental health this week - Family dinner, lunch with friend, coworker - Talk about what you learned from this book - Normalize the conversation. Break the silence.

Day 21: Attend something - City council meeting - NAMI event - Community forum - Church mental health ministry meeting - Show up in person. Be counted.

Day 22-24: Choose your lane - You can't do everything. What's YOUR lane?

- Direct support (checking on people, crisis intervention)?

- Advocacy (contacting officials, organizing)?

- Education (teaching others, sharing resources)?

- Funding (donating, fundraising)?

- Pick what fits your gifts and circumstances. Commit to that.

Day 25-27: Create accountability - Find one person doing this work with you - Check in with each other weekly - Share wins and frustrations - Don't do this alone. We're stronger together.

Day 28-30: Evaluate and adjust - What worked? What didn't?

- What can you sustain long-term?

- What needs to change?

- Make your next 30-day plan. Keep going.

This isn't a 30-day challenge that ends when the month is over.

This is building a PRACTICE. A way of living. A commitment.

After 30 days: - You'll have established daily mental health practices - You'll have made real connections in community - You'll have taken concrete advocacy actions - You'll have momentum Now you keep going. Because the work doesn't end.

Let me be honest with you about something: This work will hurt.

Not in some abstract, theoretical way. It will hurt in your chest when you hear about another death. It will hurt in your bones when you feel like you're pushing against a wall that won't move. It will hurt in your spirit when you see how little some people care.

Advocacy for Black mental health is traumatic. Especially when you're carrying your own mental health struggles while fighting for systemic change.

Here's how to keep going anyway: You cannot sustain this work if you're not taking care of yourself.

Not "self-care Sundays" where you light a candle and take a bath once a week. Real, daily, non-negotiable mental health protection.

This means: - Therapy if you can access it (and you should be able to using Chapter 5's resources) - Medication if you need it (no shame, no apology) - Daily practices from

Chapter 6 (breathing, movement, sleep, nutrition, connection) - Boundaries on how much you take in (you don't have to watch every video, read every story, attend every vigil) - Time completely away from the work (you're allowed to have joy, rest, peace) Remember: Taking care of yourself isn't selfish. It's strategic.

You can't pour from an empty cup. You can't fight for others if you're falling apart. Your wellness is part of the work, not separate from it.

This work doesn't have a finish line.

You won't wake up one day and mental health disparities will be solved.

Police violence will continue. The system will still be broken. That's the truth.

But there will be small wins. Celebrate them: - One person got connected to therapy because of you - One official responded to your email - One person showed up to the meeting you organized - One conversation changed someone's mind - One life saved - One day survived Those matter. Count them. Celebrate them.

The work is long. The wins are small. Celebrate them anyway.

You cannot do this alone.

Find: - People doing the same work (they understand in ways others can't) - People who have your back (when you need to fall apart) - People who make you laugh (joy is resistance) - People who remind you why it matters (when you forget) Join groups. Build coalitions. Create community.

Individual action matters. Collective action changes systems.

You're allowed to step back.

You're allowed to: - Take a week off from advocacy work - Skip the rally when you're exhausted - Say "I can't take this on right now"

- Protect your peace - Rest Rest isn't giving up. Rest is how you keep going.

The movement will be here when you come back. Take care of yourself first.

When it gets hard—and it will get hard—remember: Deborah Danner, who predicted her own death in an essay about police violence against people with mental illness.

Walter Wallace Jr., whose mother begged officers not to shoot her son.

Kayla Moore, shot nine times while already restrained in a hospital bed.

Andrea Clark, who died in jail because Georgia refused to expand Medicaid.

Porter Burks, shot 38 times during a mental health crisis at 20 years old.

And the ones whose names we don't know. The ones who died this week. The ones who will die next week if we don't act.

When you want to quit, remember them.

When you feel like it doesn't matter, remember them.

When you wonder if you're making a difference, remember that every action you take might be the difference between someone living and someone dying.

That's why you keep going.

You might think you're just one person. But let me tell you what one person can do: One person checking on a friend might save their life that day.

One person sharing a resource might connect someone to therapy who's been suffering in silence for years.

One person speaking at a city council meeting might be the voice that finally breaks through and leads to policy change.

One person organizing a support group might create the community that keeps five other people alive.

One person refusing to stay silent might give ten other people courage to speak up.

One person voting for mental health might be the vote that elects an official who funds mobile crisis teams that save hundreds of lives.

You are not just one person. You are one person starting a ripple that spreads wider than you'll ever see.

Remember Marcus from Oregon? 28 years old, PTSD and depression from police violence, arrested three times, no insurance, cycling between crisis and jail.

After Oregon's reforms: Got Medicaid, accessed culturally specific mobile crisis team, received trauma-focused therapy, joined peer support group, found employment, crisis-free for 18 months.

But here's what I didn't tell you: Marcus is now a peer specialist working on the mobile crisis team that helped him.

In his first year, he responded to over 100 crisis calls. He connected people to resources. He shared his story. He showed them recovery is possible.

How many of those 100 people are alive because Marcus got help?

How many are in recovery because he showed them the way?

Marcus was helped. Now he helps others. That's the ripple.

You can be someone's Marcus. And maybe someday, they'll be someone else's Marcus.

That's how movements grow. One person. One action. One ripple at a time.

Close your eyes for a minute. Imagine this: Your family member is having a mental health crisis. You call for help.

Within 15 minutes, a mobile crisis team arrives. No police. No guns.

Just trained mental health professionals and a peer specialist who's been through crisis themselves and knows what it feels like.

They're calm. They're kind. They speak your language—culturally and literally. They see your loved one as a person in pain, not a criminal to control.

They assess the situation. They de-escalate with patience and skill. They create a safety plan. They connect to follow-up care. Your loved one goes to a crisis stabilization center—not jail, not ER—a comfortable place designed for healing where they can stay for 48 hours and get connected to ongoing treatment.

No one gets arrested. No one gets shot. Everyone survives. Your loved one gets help.

Three days later, they see a therapist. Not six weeks from now. Not after they've hit rock bottom. Three days.

The therapist is culturally competent, trauma-informed, and actually understands what it means to be Black in America. They develop a treatment plan that honors your loved one's faith, their culture, their whole life—not just symptoms to eliminate.

The therapy is covered by insurance. Or Medicaid. Or a sliding scale the therapist offers because mental health centers are fully funded and can afford to see people who can't pay.

There's a peer support group meeting that week. Your loved one goes.

Meets other Black folks dealing with similar struggles. Finds community.

Realizes they're not alone.

Six months later, your loved one is in recovery. Working. Living.

Thriving. Not just surviving.

And no one had to die for this to happen.

Everything I just described? That's happening in Portland for many people.

Not for everyone. Not perfectly. But it's happening.

Mobile crisis teams. Three-day wait times. Culturally specific care. Peer support. Recovery.

60% reduction in police shootings of people with mental health crises in Portland's Black community.

That means people who would be dead are alive. That's real. That's what's possible.

Now imagine that in your city. Your county. Your state. Everywhere.

That's what we're building. That's the vision.

A world where mental health crises don't end in death. Where asking for help doesn't require calculating risk. Where recovery is possible and supported.

We're not there yet. But Oregon proved we can get there.

The question is: How many people will die while we wait for everyone else to catch up?

Your action determines that answer.

Reading this book doesn't change anything. Your commitment does.

Take out your phone or grab a piece of paper. Write this down:

MY COMMITMENT TO MENTAL HEALTH JUSTICE

I, _____, having learned the truth about mental health disparities in Black communities, make the following commitments: Personal Healing: I commit to: _____ (one daily mental health practice from Chapter 6) Community Support: I commit to checking on _____ (name one person) at least weekly.

Advocacy Action: I commit to _____ (one specific advocacy action from Sections 1-2) Sustained Engagement: I commit to staying in this fight for _____ (time period—30 days, 6 months, one year, forever) My Why: I'm doing this because: _____ Starting: Today's date: _____ Accountability: I will share this commitment with: _____ (one person who will hold you accountable) Fill that out. Right now.

Don't just think about it. Write it down. Make it real.

Commitments written down and shared with others are commitments you actually keep.

Now do something uncomfortable: Tell someone.

Text that accountability person. Post on social media. Tell a friend. Write it on your bathroom mirror.

Make it public. Make it real. Make it impossible to back out quietly.

Because here's what I know about human nature: We can easily disappoint ourselves. It's much harder to disappoint others who are counting on us.

Make this commitment to someone else. Let them hold you to it.

There are thousands of people across this country fighting the same fight you're about to join.

The Andrea Clark Coalition in Georgia. The Justice for Porter Burks movement in Detroit. NAMI chapters in every state. Mental Health America affiliates in communities everywhere. Black Emotional & Mental Health Collective organizing nationally. Boris Lawrence Henson Foundation breaking stigma. The Loveland Foundation funding therapy.

Barbershop mental health initiatives. Faith community partnerships.

Peer support networks. Community health workers. Culturally specific crisis teams.

People showing up at city council meetings. Organizing rallies.

Making phone calls. Knocking on doors. Testifying at hearings.

Training providers. Funding programs. Saving lives.

You're joining a movement that's already in motion. You don't have to build this from scratch. You just have to show up.

National Organizations (Working Everywhere): NAMI (National Alliance on Mental Illness) - nami.org - Find local chapter - Join support group - Attend advocacy events - Get trained as peer specialist BEAM (Black Emotional & Mental Health Collective) beam.community - Training and movement building - Grant-making for Black-led initiatives - Resources and tools Boris Lawrence Henson Foundation - borislhensonfoundation.org - Fighting stigma in Black communities - Funding therapy - Training providers The Loveland Foundation - thelovelandfoundation.org - Funding therapy for Black women and girls - Building healing spaces Mental Health America - mhanational.org - Policy advocacy - Screening tools - Local affiliates Local Action (In Your Community): Find your NAMI chapter: Search "NAMI [your city/state]"

Join your local mental health coalition: Most cities have one. Google "[your city] mental health coalition" or "[your county] behavioral health board"

Connect with Black-led organizations in your area: Search "[your city] Black mental health" or "[your city] African American mental health"

Start attending city council meetings: They're public. You can speak during public comment. Use your voice.

You don't have to create infrastructure. It exists. You just have to show up.

Maybe you picked up this book because you're not okay.

Maybe you're struggling with depression, anxiety, PTSD, bipolar disorder, or something else that's making every day feel impossible.

Maybe you're reading about advocacy and thinking, "I can barely get out of bed. How am I supposed to change systems?"

Listen to me carefully: Your first responsibility is to yourself. Your own healing. Your own survival.

You cannot save anyone else if you don't save yourself first.

Everything I've written in this chapter about taking action, about advocacy, about fighting for change—all of that can wait if you're in crisis.

If you're having suicidal thoughts right now: - Call 988 (Suicide & Crisis Lifeline) - Text HOME to 741741 (Crisis Text Line) - Call 1-866-244-7470 (Black Mental Health

Hotline) - Go to your nearest emergency room - Call someone you trust Do that first. Right now. Before you read another word.

If you're struggling but not in immediate crisis: - Chapter 5 has resources for finding help - Chapter 6 has daily practices you can start today - Your healing journey is your contribution right now You don't owe anyone advocacy work. You don't owe anyone organizing. You don't owe anyone anything except taking care of yourself.

Your survival is resistance. Your healing is revolutionary. Your recovery is victory.

When you're stronger, if you choose to join the fight, we'll be here.

But right now, your only job is to survive. To heal. To get through today.

And that's enough. You are enough.

This book is about mental health in Black communities. But mental health crisis doesn't only affect us.

Veterans returning from combat with PTSD are struggling. First responders—police, firefighters, EMTs, paramedics—carrying trauma from what they witness every day. Survivors of sexual assault, domestic violence, accidents, natural disasters.

Trauma is trauma. Pain is pain. Suffering is suffering.

Yes, Black communities face unique and compounding challenges— racism, discrimination, systemic barriers, historical trauma.

Everything in this book is true and necessary.

But the broader truth is this: Our mental health system fails

EVERYONE.

It fails the veteran who waited eight months for a VA appointment while his PTSD spiraled.

It fails the firefighter who saw too many bodies and started drinking to sleep at night.

It fails the sexual assault survivor who couldn't afford trauma therapy.

It fails the person in a rural area where the nearest psychiatrist is 100 miles away.

The systems that fail Black communities are the same systems failing millions of others.

My next project is a guide specifically for PTSD—for everyone.

Military veterans and active-duty service members. Police officers, firefighters, EMTs, and paramedics. Survivors of assault, abuse, accidents, and disasters. Anyone carrying trauma the system overlooks or excludes.

Because here's what I know from 15+ years of lived experience navigating mental health systems: Trauma doesn't discriminate. It doesn't care about your race, gender, age, or background. We are all susceptible to pain and hurt from experiences that overwhelm our capacity to cope.

I'm a survivor. I've been in the trenches. I've fought through the barriers. I've learned what works and what doesn't.

And I want to help others not just survive, but THRIVE.

That's my mission. That's my calling. That's why I write.

Not just to document problems, but to provide solutions. Not just to raise awareness, but to create pathways to healing. Not just to survive, but to help others thrive.

Coming soon from Breaking Ranks Books.

This will be a practical, no-nonsense guide for: - Veterans and service members transitioning back to civilian life - First responders carrying the weight of what they've witnessed - Survivors of trauma who can't afford years of therapy - Family members supporting loved ones with PTSD - Anyone who's been told to "just get over it" and knows it's not that simple Real strategies. Evidence-based approaches. Lived experience wisdom.

Because we deserve more than "thank you for your service" and a broken VA system.

We deserve more than "heroes work here" signs and no mental health support.

We deserve more than awareness campaigns and no actual treatment.

We deserve healing. We deserve thriving. We deserve lives worth living.

That's what I'm building next. That's the next fight.

Let me tell you something personal.

I'm not a researcher sitting in an ivory tower studying Black mental health from a distance.

I'm not a politician making promises I don't have to keep.

I'm not a consultant getting paid to write reports no one will read.

I'm a Black man who has lived this. Who continues to live this.

I'm a 22-year veteran who saw things in Desert Storm, Haiti, Bosnia, and Kosovo that still visit me at night.

I'm someone who has navigated the mental health system for over 15 years. Who knows what it's like to be dismissed, misdiagnosed, medicated without proper evaluation, told my trauma wasn't real or wasn't "that bad."

I know what it's like to be strong for everyone else while falling apart inside.

I know what it's like to finally ask for help and get handed pills instead of therapy.

I know what it's like to be seen as a threat instead of a person in pain.

I wrote this book because I needed it when I was at my lowest and it didn't exist.

I wrote this book because Deborah Danner should be alive.

I wrote this book because someone needs to tell the truth about what's killing us and what can save us.

I wrote this book because I survived, and I don't want to be the only one.

This isn't just information. This is life and death.

Every statistic in this book represents a real person. Every barrier I described has killed someone. Every policy failure has a body count.

When I tell you Black adults are less likely to receive mental health treatment, that's my cousins, my neighbors, my community.

When I tell you police kill people having mental health crises, that could have been me. That could be you. That could be someone you love.

When I tell you the system is broken, I'm not speaking theoretically.

I'm speaking from the scars.

This book is my attempt to turn pain into purpose. To transform survival into service. To make sure my struggle—and the struggle of millions like me—means something.

But it only means something if YOU do something with it.

"Until the well runs dry, we must take care of each other."

That's been my message throughout this book. That's been my life's mission.

The well is running dry for too many of us. But it doesn't have to.

We can refill it. Together.

Every person who gets connected to therapy refills the well a little.

Every mobile crisis team that saves a life instead of ending one refills the well a little.

Every policy change, every funded program, every reduced barrier refills the well a little.

Every act of community care, every check-in, every resource shared refills the well a little.

You, taking action, refills the well.

We can do this. We are doing this. In Oregon. In Denver. In communities where people refused to accept death as inevitable.

We can refill the well. But only if we work together.

Only if you refuse to go back to not knowing.

Only if you commit to being part of the solution.

So here we are. The end of the book. The beginning of your commitment.

Eight chapters. One journey. From human faces to historical trauma to current crisis to deadly systems to accessible resources to healing practices to collective power to this moment right here.

You know now.

You know the history. You know the barriers. You know what's killing us and what can save us.

You know Deborah's name. Walter's name. Kayla's name. Andrea's name. Porter's name.

You can't unknow them.

You can't pretend the system isn't broken.

You can't act surprised when the next person dies.

You know.

And knowing creates responsibility.

So what are you going to do about it?

That's not a rhetorical question. That's THE question.

Are you going to: - Close this book and go back to your life unchanged?

- Feel sad for a while and then forget?

- Share on social media and call it activism?

Or are you going to: - Save those crisis numbers in your phone today?

- Check on someone this week?

- Show up to one meeting this month?

- Make one call to one official?

- Join one organization?

- Start one daily practice?

- Make one commitment and keep it?

Your answer determines whether this book was words on a page or a catalyst for change.

Your answer determines whether Deborah, Walter, Kayla, Andrea, and Porter died for nothing or whether their deaths forced us to build the world they deserved to live in.

Your answer determines whether the next person in crisis lives or dies.

That's the weight of what I'm asking you to carry.

That's the responsibility that comes with knowing.

But here's what I want you to know: You're not carrying it alone.

Thousands of us are in this fight. Some of us have been fighting for years.

Some are just starting, like you.

We're building a movement. We're forcing change. We're refilling the well.

And we need you.

Not the perfect version of you. Not the version that has it all figured out. Not the version that's fully healed and completely ready.

We need YOU. Right now. As you are. With whatever you can give.

One person. One action. One commitment at a time.

That's how the well gets refilled.

That's how we win.

The well is still running. But it doesn't have to run dry.

Not for you. Not for your community. Not for the generations coming after you.

You have everything you need: - The knowledge (this book) - The resources (Chapter 5) - The tools (Chapter 6) - The strategies (Chapter 7) - The commitment (your answer to the question) Now you just have to begin.

Do one thing today. Then one thing tomorrow. Then one thing the day after that.

Check on your people. Share the resources. Use your voice. Show up.

Stay committed.

Take care of yourself while fighting for others. Heal while helping.

Survive while building the world where everyone can thrive.

That's the work. That's the mission. That's the movement.

Welcome to the fight.

Until the well runs dry, we take care of each other.

Let's make sure it doesn't.

To the reader who made it this far: Thank you. For reading. For listening. For considering the weight of what I've shared.

This book is part of my life's mission, but it's not the end of it.

Breaking Ranks Blog (big-sarge.blog) continues to be my platform for advocacy, for truth-telling, for keeping the conversation going beyond these pages.

Breaking Ranks Books will continue publishing work that matters—work that tells our stories, that documents our struggles, that provides real solutions to real problems.

My next project—the PTSD guide—is already in progress. Because mental health advocacy doesn't stop with one community, one issue, one book.

We're all fighting for the same thing: a world where asking for help doesn't require calculating risk, where trauma is treated with compassion instead of violence, where everyone—regardless of race, gender, age, or background— has access to the healing they deserve.

I'm a survivor working to help others thrive.

That's my mission. That's my calling. That's my commitment.

I hope it becomes yours too.

Until the well runs dry, we take care of each other.

Let's make sure it doesn't.

Wayne A. Ince Senior Master Sergeant (Ret.), U.S. Air Force Author, Advocate, Survivor Breaking Ranks Books Big-Sarge.blog

For resources, updates, and to join the movement: Visit big-sarge.blog

Follow Breaking Ranks Books Contact: info@breakingranksblog

If you or someone you know is in crisis: Call 988 (Suicide & Crisis Lifeline) Text HOME to 741741 (Crisis Text Line) Call 1-866-244-7470 (Black Mental Health Hotline)** Your life matters. Your healing matters. Your voice matters.

The work continues. Join us.

COMING SOON FROM BREAKING RANKS BOOKS:

"THE UNSEEN MARCH: A Practical Guide to Managing PTSD for Veterans, First Responders, and Trauma Survivors"

By Wayne A. Ince Because trauma is trauma. Because we all deserve to thrive, not just survive. Because the march continues, even when no one sees it.

Breaking Ranks Books: Publishing Truth. Building Hope. Changing Lives.

MENTAL HEALTH CRISIS RESOURCES

IF YOU ARE IN IMMEDIATE DANGER, CALL 911

IMMEDIATE CRISIS SUPPORT (24/7)

988 Suicide & Crisis Lifeline Call or Text: 988 • Confidential support for people in distress • Prevention and crisis resources • Available 24/7 in English and Spanish Crisis Text Line Text "HOME" to 741741 • Free, confidential support via text message • Trained crisis counselors available 24/7 Veterans Crisis Line Call: 988, then press 1 | Text: 838255 Chat: VeteransCrisisLine.net/Chat • Specialized support for veterans and their families • Staff includes veterans and family members

SPECIALIZED SUPPORT LINES (24/7)

SAMHSA National Helpline: 1-800-662-HELP (4357) Mental health and substance abuse treatment referrals Black Mental Health Alliance: 410-338-2642 Culturally competent mental health support Disaster Distress Helpline: 1-800-985-5990 or Text "TalkWithUs" to 66746 Support for emotional distress related to disasters NAMI Helpline: 1-

800-950-NAMI (6264) Monday-Friday, 10am-10pm ET |
Information, referrals, and support

FIRST RESPONDER RESOURCES

Copline (Police Officers): 1-800-267-5463
Confidential helpline for law enforcement officers Fire/EMS
Helpline: 1-888-731-FIRE (3473) Share the Load Program
for firefighters and EMS Safe Call Now (All First
Responders): 206-459-3020 Confidential help for public
safety employees and their families

ADDITIONAL SUPPORT

National Domestic Violence Hotline: 1-800-799-7233
or Text "START" to 88788 National Sexual Assault Hotline:
1-800-656-HOPE (4673) Trevor Project (LGBTQ+ Youth): 1-
866-488-7386 or Text "START" to 678678 Trans Lifeline:
877-565-8860

ONLINE RESOURCES

• MentalHealth.gov - Information and treatment
locator • Psychology Today - Find a therapist directory •
NAMI.org - Support groups and education • Big-Sarge.Blog -
Veteran and first responder mental health advocacy

REMEMBER:

✓ You are not alone ✓ Help is available ✓ Healing is possible ✓ Asking for help is a sign of strength, not weakness If you are experiencing a mental health emergency, do not hesitate to call 911 or go to your nearest emergency room.

This resource sheet is provided as a public service. Please keep it accessible and share it with others who may need support.

BIBLIOGRAPHY AND REFERENCES

This bibliography consolidates all sources cited throughout the manuscript.

Mental Health Crisis and Help-Seeking (2024-2025) - Anderson, A., Eisenberg, M.D., Kennedy-Hendricks, A., Castrucci, B.C., Galea, S., & Ettman, C.K. (2025).

Mental health crises and help-seeking among US adults in 2024-2025. *Health Affairs Scholar*, 3(9), qxaf166.

https://doi.org/10.1093/haschl/qxaf166 - Anderson, A., Spivak, S., & Kennedy-Hendricks, A. (2025). Availability of Mobile Crisis Services in Mental Health Facilities.

JAMA Network Open, 8(2), e2461321. doi:10.1001/jamanetworkopen.2024.61321 Mobile Crisis Teams and Crisis Response –

National Research Institute (NRI). (2024). *Someone to Respond: Mobile Crisis Teams (MCTs)*. https://www.nri-inc.org/profiles - SAMHSA. (2024). *National Survey of Mobile Crisis Teams*.

https://988crisissystemshelp.samhsa.gov - Government Accountability Office (GAO). (2025).

Behavioral Health: Federal Activities to Support Crisis Response Services (GAO-25-107586).

Trauma-Informed Therapy and Treatment Approaches - Yadav, G., McNamara, S., & Gunturu, S. (2024). Trauma-Informed Therapy. *StatPearls*. Updated August 16, 2024. Treasure Island (FL): StatPearls Publishing.

- Burback, L., et al. (2025). Evolving psychotherapeutic approaches for PTSD. *Psychiatry and Clinical Psychopharmacology*, 35(Suppl. 1), S152S167.

- Cohen, J.A., Mannarino, A.P., & Deblinger, E. (2024). *The Trauma-Focused Cognitive Behavioral Therapy (TF-CBT): At-A-Glance*. Los Angeles, CA & Durham, NC: National Center for Child Traumatic Stress.

Racial Trauma and Healing - Williams, M.T., et al. (2022). An evidence-based approach for treating stress and trauma due to racism. *Cognitive and Behavioral Practice*, 30(4), 565–588. doi:10.1016/j.cbpra.2022.07.001 –

Williams, M.T., et al. (2025). Treating Racial Trauma: The Methodology of a Randomized Controlled Trial of the Healing Racial Trauma Protocol.

Healthcare, 15(7), 856. https://doi.org/10.3390/healthcare15070856 Mental Health in Black Communities - Elhabashy, M., Adzrago, D., & Williams, F. (2025). Psychological distress among US-born and non-US-born Black or African American adults in the US. *JAMA Network Open*, 8(4), e256558.

- Johns Hopkins Bloomberg School of Public Health. (2025). *Mental Health Crisis Hits Nearly 1 in 10 U.S. Adults*. Press release, September 3, 2025.

Crisis Hotlines and Help-Seeking Behaviors - Springer Nature. (2026). Bridging the Crisis Gap: A Scoping Review of Psychological Distress and Help-Seeking Behaviors in Black Americans Using Crisis Hotlines. *Community Mental Health Journal*.

Therapy Trends and Modalities - Zencare. (2025). *In Private Practice: The State of Mental Health Report 2025*. Blog post analyzing 2025 therapy trends.

EMDR and Trauma Treatment - PESI. (2024). *EMDR Training for Clinicians*. Professional training materials and research compilation.

- Alter Behavioral Health. (2025). *Trauma Treatment Modalities: Effective Approaches*. November 14, 2025.

Medicaid and Crisis Funding - Milbank Memorial Fund. (2025). Mobile Crisis Teams and Medicaid Funding:

Advancing Behavioral Health Crisis Response Across the United States. June 12, 2025.

Police Response and Mental Health - Marcus, N., & Stergiopoulos, V. (2024). Re-examining mental health crisis intervention: A rapid review comparing outcomes across police, coresponder and non-police models. *Journal of Mental Health*.

Federal Resources - Substance Abuse and Mental Health Services Administration (SAMHSA).

(2025). *National Guidelines for Crisis Care*. Updated 2025.

- National Institute of Mental Health (NIMH). (2024). *Mental Health Statistics*.

- Centers for Disease Control and Prevention (CDC). (2024). *Mental Health Data and Statistics*.

State and Local Studies - RAND Corporation. (2020). *Economic Analysis of Mental Health Investment in LA County*.

- Oregon Health Authority. (2018-2022). *Mental Health Legislation Outcomes and Impact Assessment*.

Historical and Cultural Context - Washington, H.A. (2006). *Medical Apartheid: The Dark History of Medical

Experimentation on Black Americans from Colonial Times to the Present*.Doubleday.

- hooks, b. (1993). *Sisters of the Yam: Black Women and Self-Recovery*.South End Press.

- DeGruy, J. (2017). *Post Traumatic Slave Syndrome: America's Legacy of Enduring Injury and Healing*. Joy DeGruy Publications.

Mental Health and African American Communities - Boyd, R. (2022). Multiple works on anti-Black racism and health equity. Various publications.

- Williams, M.T. (Multiple years). Extensive body of work on racism-related stress and trauma.

National Organizations - National Alliance on Mental Illness (NAMI). www.nami.org - Mental Health America (MHA). www.mhanational.org - Black Emotional and Mental Health Collective (BEAM).

www.beam.community - Boris Lawrence Henson Foundation. www.borislhensonfoundation.org - The Loveland Foundation. www.thelovelandfoundation.org Therapy and Provider Directories –

Therapy for Black Girls. www.therapyforblackgirls.com –

Therapy for Black Men. www.therapyforblackmen.org – Black Mental Health Alliance. www.blackmentalhealth.com –

Inclusive Therapists. www.inclusivetherapists.com - Melanin & Mental Health. @melaninandmentalhealth Specialized Services –

Sista Afya (Mental Health for Black Women) - The Confess Project (Black Men's Mental Health) –

National Queer and Trans Therapists of Color Network (NQTTCN) Crisis Services –

988 Suicide & Crisis Lifeline. www.988lifeline.org - Crisis Text Line. www.crisistextline.org –

SAMHSA National Helpline. 1-800-662-HELP (4357) Major Publications - Chicago Tribune. (2022). "Lack of resources and stigma are barriers to Black mental health care."

- Johns Hopkins University. (2025). Research on mental health crisis prevalence.

- The Sojourner's Truth. (2025). "Black Mental Health and Surviving 2025."

Digital Publications - Medium.com (various authors on Black mental health) - Vocal.Media (mental health advocacy content) –

FunTimes Magazine. (2023). "African American mental health struggles and challenges."

Training and Certification Programs - Mental Health First Aid USA - Crisis Intervention Team (CIT) Training - EMDR International Association - TF-CBT Web.

www.tfcbt.org Healthcare Organizations - American Psychological Association (APA) - American Psychiatric Association - National Association of Social Workers

(NASW) - Association of Black Psychologists (ABPsi) Blogs and Personal Narratives - Breaking Ranks Blog.

www.breakingranksblog.com (www.big-sarge.blog) - Various personal testimony from community members, survivors, and advocates Faith-Based Resources - African American church mental health ministries –

Faith community partnerships documented in various communities Local Initiatives –

CAHOOTS (Eugene, Oregon). 30+ years of program data - STAR Program (Denver, Colorado). Program outcomes 2020-present - Mental Health SF (San Francisco).

Citywide program data - Oregon comprehensive mental health reform (2018-present) Federal Legislation - Mental Health Parity and Addiction Equity Act –

Affordable Care Act (ACA) provisions related to mental health - American Rescue Plan Act (ARPA) - Mental Health provisions State Policies - Medicaid expansion policies (various states) - Crisis response legislation (various states) –

Mental health court programs Primary Sources - PubMed/NCBI (National Center for Biotechnology Information) - PsycINFO - Google Scholar- JSTOR

Specialized Databases - SAMHSA's Evidence-Based Practices Resource Center - National Registry of Evidence-based Programs and Practices (NREPP) Technology and Telehealth –

Various telehealth platforms (BetterHelp, Talkspace, etc.) - referenced for accessibility options - Mental health apps designed for/with Black users Barbershop and Beauty Salon Initiatives –

Various community-based programs integrating mental health awareness in traditional Black community spaces Peer Support Programs - Multiple peer-run organizations and recovery programs –

Peer specialist certification programs Medical Ethics - Tuskegee Syphilis Study documentation - Henrietta Lacks case studies –

Historical medical experimentation records Civil Rights Era - Documentation of mental health treatment during segregation –

Historical trauma research Statistics and Demographics - U.S. Census Bureau data - CDC WONDER database –

SAMHSA National Survey on Drug Use and Health (NSDUH) - Behavioral Risk Factor Surveillance System (BRFSS) Lived Experience - Testimony from individuals with mental health challenges –

U.S. Department of Health and Human Services, Office of Minority Health.

(2025). Mental Health in Black/African Americans. Retrieved from https://minorityhealth.hhs.gov/mental-and-behavioral-health-blackafricanamericans Substance Abuse and Mental Health Services Administration (SAMHSA).

(2025). Results from the 2024 National Survey on Drug Use and Health: Mental health detailed tables. U.S. Department of Health and Human Services.

The Sojourner's Truth. (2025, April 3). Black Mental Health and Surviving 2025. Retrieved from https://wordpress.thetruthtoledo.com/index.php/2025/04/03/black-mentalhealth-and-surviving-2025/ National Alliance on Mental Illness (NAMI). (2025, November 4).

Black/African American mental health. Retrieved from https://www.nami.org/your-journey/identity-and-cultural-dimensions/blackafrican-american/ National Association for the Advancement of Colored People (NAACP). (2025, January 30).

Addressing the mental and behavioral health care needs of the Black community. Retrieved from https://naacp.org/resources/addressing-mental-and-behavioral-health-careneeds-black-community University of Michigan School of Public Health. (2024, April 13).

Bridging the gap to address Black mental health disparities. Retrieved from https://sph.umich.edu/pursuit/2024posts/black-mental-health-disparities2024.html Kaiser Family Foundation (KFF). (2023, August 14).

Racial and ethnic disparities in mental health care: Findings from the KFF survey of racism, discrimination and health. Retrieved from https://www.kff.org/racial-equityand-health-policy/racial-and-ethnic-disparities-in-mental-health-carefindings-from-the-kff-survey-of-racism-discrimination-and-health/ PBS NewsHour. (2024, July 25).

Black Americans struggle with lack of mental health access. Retrieved from https://www.pbs.org/video/troublingtrend-1721940985/ Wake Forest University. (2024, November 14).

Black mental health: Statistics, resources and services for the Black community. Retrieved from https://counseling.online.wfu.edu/blog/black-mental-health-resources McLean Hospital. (2024).

Black Mental Health Matters: Awareness, access, and action. Retrieved from https://www.mcleanhospital.org/essential/blackmental-health

Family member accounts - Survivor stories (names changed or used with permission) Professional Consultations - Conversations with therapists, psychiatrists, and mental health professionals –

Discussions with community organizers and advocates - Input from peer specialists and recovery coaches This bibliography represents sources consulted, cited, or referenced throughout "Until the Well Runs Dry: Mental Health in the African American Community."

Some sources provided background context and informed the author's understanding, while others are directly cited in specific chapters.

The most current data available as of 2025 was prioritized, with particular attention to research published in 2024-2025 to ensure contemporary relevance.

Where specific individuals' stories are shared, names have been changed to protect privacy except in cases of public record (such as widely reported deaths involving police encounters) or where individuals have given explicit permission for their stories to be shared.

The author, Wayne A. Ince, draws extensively on 15+ years of personal experience navigating mental health systems, 22 years of military service, and ongoing advocacy work through Breaking Ranks Blog and Breaking Ranks Books.

For the most current resources and ongoing updates: - Visit: www.big-sarge.blog (Breaking Ranks Blog) - Follow: Breaking Ranks Books for new publications –

Crisis Support: 988 (call or text), 1-866-244-7470 (Black Mental Health Hotline) Last Updated: January 2026

Compiled by: Wayne A. Ince, Author For: Until the Well Runs Dry: Mental Health in the African American Community Publisher: Breaking Ranks Books

ABOUT THE AUTHOR

Wayne A. Ince served 22 years in the U.S. Air Force with deployments to Desert Storm, Haiti, Bosnia, and Kosovo. Drawing from 15+ years of navigating mental health systems, he founded Breaking Ranks Books and the Breaking Ranks Blog to advocate for mental health awareness, particularly for veterans, first responders, and marginalized communities.

COMING SOON FROM BREAKING RANKS BOOKS:

"The Unseen March: A Practical Guide to Managing PTSD"

By Wayne A. Ince Expected 2026

www.ingramcontent.com/pod-product-compliance
Lightning Source LLC
Chambersburg PA
CBHW022332280326
41934CB00006B/610